Stories that heal

64 creative visualisations for use in therapy

Roger & Christine Day

Brook Creative Therapy

Copyright Roger & Christine Day 2011

First published in 2011 by Brook Creative Therapy

All rights reserved. No part of this publication may be reproduced or transmitted in any form or by any means, electronic or mechanical, including photocopy, recording or any information storage and retrieval system, without permission in writing from the publisher. Pages may be photocopied for therapeutic, supervisory and training use only.

Published by:

Brook Creative Therapy, Brook Cottage, 16 Burnside, Rugby, Warwickshire CV22 6AX, UK

Details of how to order further copies can be obtained by emailing brookcreativetherapy@gmail.com

About the authors

Roger Day
Certified Transactional Analyst, Psychotherapist and Play Therapy specialist
For many years Roger has been a trainer and supervisor specialising in children and families. Now retired, he lives in Rugby, Warwickshire.

Christine Day
European Adult Teaching Certificate, Nursery Nurse Examination Board (NNEB), Diploma in Counselling, Certificate in Counselling Skills
Christine is a qualified nursery nurse. In addition to successfully raising four children, over the years she has added play and creativity specialisms to her nursery skills. Christine lives with Roger in Rugby, Warwickshire.

Books by Roger & Christine Day:

Matryoshkas in Therapy: Creative ways to use Russian dolls with clients
Creative Anger Expression
Creative Therapy in the Sand: Using sandtray with clients

Christine & Roger Day have also published the following books in CD-ROM form:

Body Awareness: 64 bodywork activities for therapy (2008/2011)
Therapeutic Adventure: 64 activities for therapy outdoors (2008/2011)
Stories that Heal: 64 creative visualisations for use in therapy (2011)

Brook Creative Therapy, Brook Cottage, 16 Burnside, Rugby CV22 6AX, UK

Contents

Introduction

Drawing out the story
    The winter garden
    Who am I?
    A friend indeed
    Puzzle of my life
    Digital image
    Journey into space
    Through the tunnel
    Kite flying

Writing the vision
    The room
    This is your life
    My cave
    In the cafe
    Writing a letter
    Song of life
    What's in a name?
    Looking at life differently

Shaping the event
    The mountain climb
    The lonely ballerina
    Fly away
    Burning rubber
    The prison cell
    A wedding
    Uncharted waters
    Cliff walk

Moving through
    Reaching towards the sun
    Rising on eagle's wings
    The littlest dolphin

    A growing child
    Swimming with dolphins
    Race of life
    In touch with your body
    Wild swimming

Bringing colour to the story
    The cloud
    Colours of anxiety
    I'm a survivor
    The colour of music
    Volcanic eruption
    Two apples
    After the event
    A child of your choice

The vision expressed
    Your life on film
    A bus journey
    Call the lifeboat
    Carnival parade
    Lost in the forest
    Lone navigation
    Helicopter trip
    Hidden treasure

Collage and 3D creation
    The waterfall
    Helium balloons
    Tickets, please
    Buddies
    Treasure!
    An invitation
    A trip to the beach
    Gift of life

Shaping the visualisation
    Journey of life
    Turmoil to relaxation

A mighty oak
On top of the world
At the party
A gift for me
Taking care of yourself
The visitor

Sources and references

Introduction

Visualise: 'Make visible to the eye. Give outward and visible form to mental image. Call up distinct mental picture of thing imagined or formerly seen' (Concise Oxford Dictionary).

'A therapeutic story uses the realm of the imagination and metaphor rather than cognition or literal speech' (Wilson & Ryan, 1992/2005, page 9).

Visualisations and therapeutic stories can be very powerful for working with clients. When they are combined with a therapeutic activity they can be even more effective and empowering.

Clients form their own mental picture and subsequently their own decisions.

A visualisation or therapeutic story is a guide, not something fixed. It is a way of suggesting options or asking questions so that clients can come to their own conclusions about what is being said.

Visualisations and therapeutic stories can be used for relaxation, looking at problems in a different way or seeing life more positively. Indeed, they can help clients to make redecisions that lead to major therapeutic changes.

One of the most powerful visualisations, that we use regularly in our work with both adults and children, is called the Rosebush Visualisation (Allan, 1992). In brief, this involves inviting the client to become a rosebush, imagining the kind of bush, the type of flowers, the form of protection and nourishment, and the rosebush's location. Clients then draw or paint their imagined rosebush and discuss it with the therapist. This visualisation can be used for assessment or for therapeutic change.

Our own visualisations have a similar aim. Each visualisation and therapeutic story in this book has an activity to go with it. This is to help clients think through and express what they have come to realise about themselves or their situation, past or present.

We have used eight different techniques to enhance the experience: drawing, writing, clay, movement, paint, drama, collage/3D and human sculpting. These techniques are interchangeable. A particular client may find a preference for one type of activity, such as paint. If that is the case, the therapist can adapt many of the visualisations to suit the preferred activity.

Here are some suggestions for the therapist who has little or no experience of using visualisations or therapeutic stories:

1. Double check that mobile phones are switched off. There is nothing worse than for a phone to ring in the middle of a visualisation!

2. In general it is best for the client to sit in a comfortable chair in a relaxed position. In particular scenarios, however, the instructions include getting the client to stand in a certain position, move as the story progresses or lie on the floor.

3. Deep breathing a couple of times can help the client to let go of things on his or her mind. A good technique to assist this is to invite the client to put one hand on the upper chest and one at the point of the diaphragm (the bottom of the rib cage). The client then breathes deeply, seeking to keep the upper hand still and the lower hand moving in time with the breathing.

4. Invite clients to close their eyes if they want to. Most people can access their imagination more effectively with eyes closed. A few will struggle with this and will prefer to keep their eyes open. Clients who have been abused or who have paranoid tendencies may also prefer to keep their eyes open.

5. The therapist reads the visualisation very slowly, with pauses where indicated. Keep to short, clear sentences. It is best to speak with the normal voice rather than anything mysterious or spooky. The visualisations and therapeutic stories in this book are not intended for hypnosis or for stage performance. By the therapist keeping to a normal voice,

clients can go as deeply into the visualisation as they want without persuasion or force.

6. When the visualisation is finished, give time for clients to come back to the here and now. Instructions for this are included for each story/visualisation. You may develop your own ritual. The idea is that the client is given time to return from the visualisation to the reality of the therapy room. Make sure clients open their eyes and engage in some kind of transition. This could consist of focusing on an object in the room, putting feet firmly on the floor, turning around or saying their name and today's date.

Enjoy using visualisations and therapeutic stories with your clients. Consider writing your own stories for the individual needs of clients. Finally, if possible, tell us know how you have used this book in helping to use stories that heal.

Roger & Christine Day
October 2011

12

Drawing out the story

Introduction

One of the most popular and effective ways of reflecting on a story or visualisation is by the client drawing it. It can be a great release for clients, first to see the mental picture, then to put it on paper. It can be very therapeutic, bringing concrete understanding of the visualisation.

Drawing is such a natural thing for a child to do. Give him or her a pencil, pen or some coloured felt-tips and that is all that is needed to start the process.

For an adult, drawing can be extremely difficult. Many people have grown up with the belief that they simply can't draw. Perhaps they were told this at school or at home. They might have come to the conclusion by comparing themselves with other people.

One of us (Roger) spent years telling people publicly and rather dismissively: 'My drawings are like those of a four-year-old.' Then one day he linked this with the fact that many of his important positive life-script decisions were made when he was four. Now he can declare proudly: 'I draw just like the four-year-old hero in me!'

Clients, too, can overcome their reluctance and start to enjoy what they draw.

A good way to start clients drawing is by inviting them to do what is known by psychologists as the House-Person-Tree projective technique. Originally developed by John Buck as a psychological test, it can be used effectively by counsellors and therapists.

Provide the client with pens, pencils and felt-tips and invite him or her to draw on one piece of paper a house, a person and a tree. No more instruction is needed. If the client becomes stuck, simply repeat the instruction until the task is completed.

When it is done invite the client to talk about his or drawing by asking questions such as: 'Tell me about the house,' 'Tell me about the tree', etc. Avoid interpretation. If you notice discrepancies, such as the person is far too small proportionately or too large to get in the door, point this out and wait for the client's explanation.

With drawings following stories or visualisations, follow the same pattern. Get the client to do the drawing, look at it together and then ask questions that draw out the client's answer, not your own interpretation of it.

As a variation you might consider inviting the client to do a drawing after the story/visualisation using the nondominant hand (left when the client normally uses right and right when the client is left-handed).

The winter garden

Materials needed

Paper, felt-tip pens, pencils, ballpoint pens.

Instructions

The therapist leads the visualisation:

Get into a comfortable position and close your eyes if you want to.

Come with me. We are going into the garden. (PAUSE) It is morning in the middle of winter. (PAUSE) Put warm clothes on. (PAUSE) Coat. (PAUSE) Boots. (PAUSE) Hat. (PAUSE) Scarf. (PAUSE) Gloves. (PAUSE) Feel the warmth of the fabric against your neck and cheeks. (PAUSE)

Step outside. (PAUSE)

Listen to the winter stillness. (PAUSE) Hear the crunch of your footsteps. (PAUSE) The loud, echoing sound of a solitary bird singing. (PAUSE) Listen to the sound of traffic in the distance. (PAUSE) Hear children squealing with delight at new discoveries. (PAUSE)

Stand still and look around you. (PAUSE) The thick white frost on the plants transforming the leaves. (PAUSE) The Jack Frost patterns in the puddles. (PAUSE) The thick ice in the bird bath. (PAUSE)

Look up at the sky. (PAUSE) The winter trees silhouetted against the blue in sharp contrast. (PAUSE) The trees covered in thick, white, sparkling frost. (PAUSE) Look with wonder at intricate spiders' webs, highlighted by the frost as if made with string. (PAUSE)

Take your gloves off for a moment and feel the sharp, frosty coldness of the air. (PAUSE)

Breathe deeply and experience the frosty air filling your lungs. (PAUSE) Look at your hot, steamy breath like fiery smoke from a dragon's mouth. (PAUSE)

Enjoy the peace and beauty of this frost covered wonderland. (PAUSE)

Step back indoors into the warm. (PAUSE) Take off your outdoor clothes and revel in a comforting mug of your favourite drink. (PAUSE) Enjoy the heat of the mug in your hands. (PAUSE) Savour your drink as it slips like warm silk down your throat and into your stomach. (PAUSE)

When you are ready, come back into the room, open your eyes and breathe deeply. Use the pens and paper to make a picture of your winter garden.

Objectives

This visualisation invites the client to a different form of relaxation based on the winter garden. It is a memorable place in which some clients can return in their imagination when the going gets tough.

Who am I?

Materials needed

Paper, felt-tip pens, pencils, ballpoint pens.

Instructions

The therapist leads the visualisation:

I invite you to sit comfortably, close your eyes and listen to this series of questions.

Who are you? (PAUSE) Are you extroverted or reserved? (PAUSE) Are you always rushing into things with great enthusiasm, or do you think first? (PAUSE)

Are you talkative, eager to share your own opinions? Or are you a listener, happy to hear what the other is saying? (PAUSE) Are you friendly? (PAUSE) Outgoing? (PAUSE) Or do you prefer your own company? (PAUSE)

Are you loving? (PAUSE) Are you lovable? (PAUSE) Are you always busy? (PAUSE) Or do you set limits and pace yourself? (PAUSE)

Are you tall? (PAUSE) Short? (PAUSE) Good looking? (PAUSE)

Do you take time just to relax? (PAUSE) Or is life too fast for that? (PAUSE)

Do you respond to your needs? (PAUSE) Or do you ignore the occasional headache or need to eat? (PAUSE)

Do you think people like you? (PAUSE)

When you are ready come back into this room, open your eyes and think about who you are. Then, using the pens and paper here, draw a description of yourself. When you are finished, look at your drawing and think about what you might like to change.

Objectives

This visualisation is about self-image and self-esteem. Focusing on who the person is can help in the therapeutic process. Sharing it with others can make it even more positive. If you are using this visualisation in a group, consider getting willing members of the group to share with the others who they are.

A friend indeed

Materials needed

Paper, felt-tip pens, pencils, ballpoint pens.

Instructions

The therapist leads the visualisation:

Find a comfortable position ready for this visualisation. You can close your eyes if that helps.

Where do you find your strength? (PAUSE) What is the rock you base your hope on? (PAUSE) Where do you find peace and rest? (PAUSE) Where do you find security in your life? (PAUSE)
Who do you trust with your hurts and fears? (PAUSE) Who do you turn to when you need a friend? (PAUSE) Where do you go for a source of comfort? (PAUSE)
Who supports you when you are sad? (PAUSE) Who is first to hear your good news? (PAUSE) Who can you laugh and cry with? (PAUSE)

When you are ready, come back into the room, open your eyes and draw a picture of friendship and its importance to you.

Objectives

Friendship is a vital part of what Eric Berne described as 'recognition hunger', 'the quest for special kinds of sensations which can only be supplied by another human being, or in some cases, by other animals' (Berne, 1972/75, page 41). This visualisation helps the client to focus on those external sources where help is available.

Puzzle of my life

Materials needed

Paper, felt-tip pens, pencils, ballpoint pens. Outline of jigsaw puzzle piece.

Instructions

The therapist leads the visualisation:

Get into a comfortable position and close your eyes if you would like.

I want you to imagine that you are sitting at a table. (PAUSE) Spread out on the table in front of you is a large jigsaw puzzle with a beautiful picture on it. (PAUSE)
The picture is of your life so far. (PAUSE) Stop and have a look. (PAUSE) What can you see? (PAUSE) Look at your different family members and your friends. (PAUSE) The beautiful shapes and colours that make up your life. (PAUSE)
As you look at the picture of your life, you can see happy times and sad times. (PAUSE) Times when life was difficult and times when everything was going well. (PAUSE)
Keep looking at your puzzle picture. As you look, you notice that a piece is missing. (PAUSE) What is on the missing piece? (PAUSE) What needs to be there to complete the picture? (PAUSE)

When you are ready, come back into the room, focusing on something or someone here. Now I invite you to take this piece of paper and make a picture of what is on your missing jigsaw piece.

Objectives

This fun visualisation and activity will help clients to focus on what they need still to put in place in their lives. It can be used as a contract for therapeutic change or as an assessment. It can also be used when a client has reached a stuck point and is not clear of the next stage in their therapeutic journey.

Digital image

Materials needed

Paper, felt-tip pens, pencils, ballpoint pens.

Instructions

The therapist leads the visualisation:

Get comfortable and close your eyes if you want to.

Imagine you are in a group, posing to have your photo taken. (PAUSE) Who are you with? (PAUSE) Are you at a wedding? (PAUSE) With some friends? (PAUSE) At the office party? (PAUSE) On holiday? (PAUSE)

How do you feel? (PAUSE) Are you at the front? (PAUSE) The most important figure in the middle? (PAUSE) On the edge? (PAUSE) Or hiding at the back? (PAUSE)

Are you posing in a funny way? Or standing with arms by your side? (PAUSE)

Are you happy to have your photo taken? (PAUSE) Or would you prefer to stay the other side of the camera? (PAUSE)

The photographer takes a formal shot, then takes snaps at every angle. (PAUSE) The camera is passed around and you look at the photos. (PAUSE) What do you think? (PAUSE) What are your feelings? (PAUSE)

Is that the real you? (PAUSE) Or are you hiding behind a mask? (PAUSE) What do you see as you look at yourself? (PAUSE)

When you are ready return to the room and open your eyes. Now draw an impression of yourself, showing the real you.

Objectives

The objective of this visualisation is to help clients explore the image they have of themselves. Hiding behind the crowd may be because of shyness. It may also be because of self-esteem issues. Similarly, being the centre of attention may be because of self-assurance or a way of masking the real self. Bringing these aspects to the client's attention through this visualisation may be a first step towards 'unmasking' and finding the true self.

Journey into space

Materials needed

Paper, felt-tip pens, pencils, ballpoint pens.

Instructions

The therapist leads the visualisation:

Find a comfortable position and close your eyes if you want to.

You are going on a journey into space. (PAUSE) You are sitting in the spaceship. (PAUSE) Your safety harness is in place. (PAUSE) You have checked the panel in front of you. (PAUSE) You are ready for lift-off. (PAUSE) How do you feel? (PAUSE) What are you thinking? (PAUSE)

Loud and clear the countdown echoes around you. (PAUSE) This is it. (PAUSE) Blast off. (PAUSE)

What is going through your mind? (PAUSE) Are you a pioneer? (PAUSE) Breaking barriers to the end of the galaxy? (PAUSE) Or do you feel overwhelmed, out of your depth? (PAUSE) Are you wondering: 'What am I doing here?'? (PAUSE)

It is a bumpy journey. (PAUSE) Are you exhilarated and thrilled? (PAUSE) Or frightened and queasy? (PAUSE)

Orders come through your headphones. (PAUSE) You press buttons, flip switches. (PAUSE) You steer the spaceship back to earth. (PAUSE)

You land with a bump. (PAUSE) Home at last! (PAUSE)

With relief you climb out of the simulator. Rubbing your eyes you realise you are in a shopping centre. (PAUSE)

What was that experience like? (PAUSE) And what valuable lessons did you learn about yourself? (PAUSE)

When you are ready, return to this room, open your eyes and – using your nondominant hand – draw your experience of the journey into space.

Objectives

This fun visualisation can be used to help clients discover internal resources they already have to head for adventure, face fears and overcome obstacles. It is important to prepare clients for the tough world they face outside the therapy room. Life is unfair, and it is important that clients learn to see difficulties as opportunities to conquer and learn from.

Through the tunnel

Materials needed

Paper, felt-tip pens, pencils, ballpoint pens.

Instructions

The therapist leads the visualisation:

Close your eyes if you want to and get yourself comfortable. We are going to another land.

You are in a land of devastation and destruction. (PAUSE) All around you is lifeless and empty. (PAUSE) Stumps of trees, blackened by fire, are all that is left of the once majestic forest. (PAUSE)
 In the meadows, grass and flowers are brown and brittle, as if they have not had rain in months. (PAUSE) The sky is overcast, adding to the depressing feeling about this wasteland. (PAUSE)
 Ahead in the hillside you notice a tunnel entrance. (PAUSE) It is small and insignificant yet you are sure it is a tunnel. (PAUSE) A way to leave this land of desolation. (PAUSE)
 As you get closer you notice a tiny source of light at the far end. (PAUSE) Standing on your toes you see the light at the end of the tunnel becoming clearer. (PAUSE) You notice an attractive bright green in the tiny dot of light. (PAUSE)
 You decide to walk through the tunnel. (PAUSE) What looked easy at first is proving difficult. (PAUSE) You are being showered by drips of water. (PAUSE) Looking up you notice that small stalactites have formed on the tunnel roof. (PAUSE) Beneath you is rough gravel that makes walking difficult. (PAUSE) Occasionally your feet splash into a deep puddle of water. (PAUSE) Sometimes you trip up because of some unseen obstacle. (PAUSE)

With a lot of effort you reach the halfway point. (PAUSE) Here, in almost total darkness, you encounter a pile of rocks that have fallen from the ceiling. (PAUSE) The light at the end of the tunnel seems to have gone. (PAUSE) The only way to continue is to scrabble up and over the pile of rocks. (PAUSE) As you reach the top you see the light much brighter. (PAUSE)

Climbing down the pile of rocks you continue your slow journey through the tunnel. (PAUSE) Now that you have overcome the worst obstacle you are excited to reach the end. (PAUSE)

The light is increasing in size and intensity as you walk closer. (PAUSE) The light green is now recognisable as beautiful trees and bushes near the entrance. (PAUSE)

Finally, you emerge into the full sunlight of the other end of the tunnel. (PAUSE) At first you are almost blinded by the unaccustomed light. (PAUSE) Gradually your eyes adjust and you start to look around. (PAUSE)

The land you have entered is one of the most beautiful you have ever seen. (PAUSE) It is full of life and greenery. (PAUSE) It is a place of peace and joy. (PAUSE)

You are still near the tunnel entrance so you look back through the tunnel. (PAUSE) What do you see? (PAUSE) What colour is the land you have left? (PAUSE) Has anything changed? (PAUSE) If so, what? (PAUSE)

In a moment I invite you to come back into the here and now, open your eyes and use the pens and paper we have here to draw what comes to your mind as a result of this visualisation.

Objectives

This visualisation can evoke powerful reactions in clients. Moving from a land of desolation to one of peace and joy could be seen as paralleling a script redecision. The hazards in the tunnel could be seen as the battle against old, negative patterns of thinking, feeling and behaviour. Emerging from the tunnel could be the reward for the huge effort involved. The client then looks back through the tunnel. Has the other land changed in any way? Or has the client's internal beliefs adjusted to the new place, so that the old land is put into perspective? Be prepared for plenty of follow-up therapy as a result of this visualisation.

Kite flying

Materials needed

Paper, felt-tip pens, pencils, ballpoint pens.

Instructions

The therapist leads the visualisation:

Make yourself comfortable and close your eyes if you want to.

Imagine it is a windy day. (PAUSE) You are out kite flying on a hill. (PAUSE) The wind is blustery and pulling at your clothes. (PAUSE) Sometimes it is difficult to stay on your feet. (PAUSE)
   You release your string and send the kite flying high in the sky. (PAUSE) Look at the colours as it dives and swoops high above you. (PAUSE) Feel the wind blowing the kite high in the sky. (PAUSE) Let your cares and troubles blow up into the sky with the kite and away. (PAUSE) How do you feel now? (PAUSE) What will you do now you are free of your cares? (PAUSE)
   Wind the string in and fold up your kite. (PAUSE) Walk down the hill, carefree and exhilarated. (PAUSE)

Come back into the here and now, opening your eyes. Use the pens and paper to draw your experience of releasing your cares and worries into the sky using your kite.

Objectives

This simple yet effective visualisation can help clients to anchor a way to release their cares and troubles. By bringing to mind the picture of the kite flying high in the sky, the client has a concrete way to let go of difficulties, that are then figuratively, and hopefully in reality, 'carried away'.

Writing the vision

Introduction

Writing as an activity after a visualisation can help to bring the story into the here and now. When the client uses words to express his or her feelings, it can enable the client to understand in concrete terms the issue he or she is dealing with.

Many clients find that writing their thoughts and feelings in a private diary can help them to express the inexpressible and to look at things from another perspective. For instance, many survivors prefer to write details of their abuse in a private diary that is later destroyed than to discuss those details with the therapist. In a similar way, writing down thoughts and feelings after a visualisation can enable clients to see issues in a different and positive way.

As with drawing, using the nondominant hand to write after a visualisation can help to anchor in the creative part of the brain any changes decided. Research has shown that script changes are more effective when the creative side of the brain is stimulated in this way.

The room

Materials needed

Paper, pens.

Instructions

The therapist leads the visualisation:

Sit comfortably and close your eyes if you want to. I'm taking you into a room.

This room can be a precious place from your past or your present. (PAUSE) Or it could be a room from your imagination. (PAUSE)

You are opening the door to the room. (PAUSE) This is a very special room. (PAUSE) There is no place here for worries, anxious thoughts or feelings of panic. (PAUSE) They cannot get through the door. (PAUSE)

Step inside and, if you would like to, take off your shoes. (PAUSE)

Take a look around you. (PAUSE) What do you see? (PAUSE)

Look at the decoration and furnishings. (PAUSE) Go over to the window and look at the view. (PAUSE) What do you see outside? (PAUSE)

Is the room warm and cosy? (PAUSE) Or is the window open, with a gentle breeze blowing the curtain? (PAUSE)

Are there photographs in the room? (PAUSE) Pictures of people who are important in your life? (PAUSE)

Now look at the chairs and settees. (PAUSE) Where will you sit? (PAUSE) Will you face the window and enjoy the view? (PAUSE) Will you sit looking into the fire and enjoy the flickering flames? (PAUSE)

Sit back and listen. (PAUSE) Your favourite music is playing. (PAUSE) Breathe deeply and enjoy the music. (PAUSE) Revel in the carefree atmosphere in this room.

(PAUSE) Enjoy. (PAUSE) Remember, this room is waiting in your imagination, and you are welcome to come back at any time. (PAUSE)

When you are ready, breathe deeply, open your eyes and come back into the here and now. For the next five minutes or so write a description of your special room. You can keep it to yourself or share it with me.

Objectives

This visualisation enables clients to find a safe place in their imagination where they can come at any time when things become difficult. Writing down a description of the room helps them to anchor the details of the room in their creative memory.

This is your life

Materials needed

Paper, pens.

Instructions

The therapist leads the visualisation:

If someone were to write a book about your life, what would it be called? Get comfortable, close your eyes if you would like, and we will explore this scenario.

In the book of your life what words would the author use to describe you? (PAUSE) Strong? (PAUSE) Courageous? (PAUSE) Brave? (PAUSE) Heroic? (PAUSE)

Would you be the hero or heroine of the story? (PAUSE) What would be the theme of the book? (PAUSE) How would it inspire other people who are struggling in life? (PAUSE)

What is the opening scene in the book? (PAUSE) How does the story develop? (PAUSE) What are the pitfalls? (PAUSE) And what are the highlights? (PAUSE)

What tragedies happen? (PAUSE) And what joys? (PAUSE)

How will the book end? (PAUSE) Triumphantly? (PAUSE) Suddenly? (PAUSE) Tragically? (PAUSE) Dramatically? (PAUSE) Gently? (PAUSE)

Will some issues still be unresolved or will all the loose ends be tied up? (PAUSE)

How could you change the book so that the story, contents and ending are the way you want them to be? (PAUSE)

When you are ready, come back into the room, look around and put your feet firmly on the ground. Now write a synopsis of your new story with your own unique ending. Try using your nondominant hand to write the story and anchor the changes you want.

Objectives

This visualisation will enable clients to look at their lives objectively. It will help them to become aware of where they are in life and where they are going. It also introduces the possibility of making script changes.

My cave

Materials needed

Paper, pens.

Instructions

The therapist leads the visualisation:

Get comfortable, close your eyes and enter into this story.

When it first happened I would withdraw into my cave. (PAUSE) It was dark and safe there. (PAUSE) I would withdraw from the world. (PAUSE) Nothing and nobody could reach me. (PAUSE) To me, this felt like my only hope. (PAUSE) To step back. (PAUSE) To disappear. (PAUSE)

But even when I was alone, the monsters in my imagination would come to haunt me. (PAUSE) Sleep seemed impossible and I would tremble in the darkness, wishing my cave was a reality. (PAUSE)

Events moved fast in a blur of court cases and conviction. (PAUSE) The horror of having to recount my shame over and over. (PAUSE)

Calm. (PAUSE) Those around me thought it was over. (PAUSE) Forgotten. (PAUSE) Carry on as if nothing has happened. (PAUSE) So I withdrew back to my cave. (PAUSE)

Small. (PAUSE) Dark. (PAUSE) Comforting. (PAUSE) A good strategy. (PAUSE) A necessary protection. (PAUSE)

My ten-year-old self was a master at masquerade and disguise. (PAUSE) I would smile at the party. (PAUSE) But my haunted eyes could hide nothing. (PAUSE)

Twenty years later I still withdraw to my cave. (PAUSE) Now it is decorated and looks welcoming. (PAUSE) My bedsit for one. (PAUSE) How deceptive looks can be. (PAUSE)

I need to move on. (PAUSE) To find another person I can trust with my fragile self. (PAUSE) Someone I can open up with. (PAUSE) To laugh and cry together without my overwhelming need to run back to my cave and hide. (PAUSE)

I'm learning to express myself. (PAUSE) Using creative ways to move on in life. (PAUSE) To forgive my ten-year-old for not saying no. (PAUSE) To realise that my ten-year-old had no protection. (PAUSE)

Facing the truth is not easy. (PAUSE) I have cried long and hard about that. (PAUSE)

I will move on. (PAUSE) It's a slow and sometimes painful process. (PAUSE) As the years are passing I have less need of my cave. (PAUSE) And I'm looking forward to leaving it for ever. (PAUSE) It was useful for a time, but maybe soon I will be able to step out and live. (PAUSE)

When you are ready, open your eyes and come back into the room. Then take a piece of paper and use words to make a picture of your feelings. See what positives are there, any useful thoughts or feelings that you would like to take with you in your life.

Objectives

This is a visualisation specifically for survivors of child abuse, rape and domestic violence. It could also be used with other clients who have been hurt physically or emotionally. The visualisation gives some understanding of the suffering clients may have felt as well as their need for protection. It is intended gently to show survivors the way forward into freedom.

In the cafe

Materials needed

Paper, pens.

Instructions

The therapist leads the visualisation:

Get comfortable and close your eyes if you want to. Come with me. I'm taking you to a cafe.

Where would you like to sit? (PAUSE) There are tables outside with umbrellas where people are sitting, chatting. (PAUSE) They are watching passers-by in the pedestrianised zone. (PAUSE) There are tubs of beautiful flowers dotted around the tables. (PAUSE)
    Inside it is light and airy. (PAUSE) There are interesting pictures on the walls. (PAUSE) The tables are all around the room. (PAUSE) Some tables are in the corners. (PAUSE) There customers can sit apart, watching what is going on. (PAUSE)
    Breathe deeply and smell the aroma of coffee. (PAUSE) How do you feel? (PAUSE) What are you thinking? (PAUSE)
    It is busy and friends are meeting, catching up with the latest news. (PAUSE) Who would you like to take to the cafe? (PAUSE)
    Are you enjoying the busyness? (PAUSE) Is it a friendly atmosphere? (PAUSE) How do you feel? (PAUSE) What are you thinking? (PAUSE) Are you part of what is going on? (PAUSE) Or just an onlooker? (PAUSE)
    You order a hot drink. (PAUSE) Relax and enjoy your drink. (PAUSE)

When you are ready, step out of the cafe, open your eyes and come back to the here and now. I invite you to write down your thoughts and feelings about your experience just now in the cafe.

Objectives

This visualisation is a form of relaxation in what is hopefully a familiar place. As the visualisation progresses it gives clients choices about how to build their unique scenario. Included within it are socialising and self-care. Clients are given permission to take care of themselves and to relax with friends.

Writing a letter

Materials needed

Paper, pens.

Instructions

The therapist leads the visualisation:

Make yourself comfortable and close your eyes if you want to.

If you could write a letter to someone, telling them about your life and how events have shaped your character, who would you write to? (PAUSE) What would you say? (PAUSE)
Would you tell of your hopes and dreams? (PAUSE) Times of joy? (PAUSE) Times of sadness? (PAUSE) Your successes? (PAUSE) Or your tragedies? (PAUSE)
Would you thank them for being a part of your life? (PAUSE) Or would you tell them how much they hurt you? (PAUSE)
Would you write that, despite everything that has happened, you are not going to give up? (PAUSE)
Would you tell of your determination? (PAUSE) Strengthened by adversity? (PAUSE)
Would you forgive them? (PAUSE) Or ask them to forgive you? (PAUSE)
When you are finished, you can tear the letter up. (PAUSE) How does that feel? (PAUSE)
Is this the first day of the rest of your life? (PAUSE)

When you are ready, open your eyes and come back to the room. Now, I invite you to write that letter of your visualisation. When you have finished writing it you can decide what you want to do with it.

Objectives

This visualisation empowers clients to express their feelings on paper. Clients can write and say things, bringing hurts into the light that may have been buried for many years. It is important to remember that it is the client's letter, and each client can interpret this visualisation in his or her own unique way.

Song of life

Materials needed

Paper, pens.

Instructions

The therapist leads the visualisation:

Find somewhere comfortable and close your eyes if you want to.

Listen to the song of your imagination. (PAUSE) What kind of music is it? (PAUSE) Fast? (PAUSE) Slow? (PAUSE) Classical? (PAUSE) Pop? (PAUSE) Jazz? (PAUSE) Reggae? (PAUSE) Rap? (PAUSE) Opera? (PAUSE)

How do you feel listening to it? (PAUSE) Now hear the words. (PAUSE) What is the song about? (PAUSE) Love? (PAUSE) Loss? (PAUSE) Life? (PAUSE) Sadness? (PAUSE) Success? (PAUSE) Serenity? (PAUSE)

Do you like the song? (PAUSE) Is this song touching your soul? (PAUSE) Is it full of hope and desire? (PAUSE) Or tragedy and disappointment? (PAUSE)

Are you happy with the song or would you like to change it? (PAUSE) If you decide to change it, how does it sound now? (PAUSE)

Listen for a little while longer. (PAUSE) Feel the music. (PAUSE) Hear the words. (PAUSE) Respond to the rhythm of the drums. (PAUSE) Embrace the words as your own. (PAUSE)

Take this song with you as you go on in life. (PAUSE)

When you are ready, open your eyes and come back to the here and now with your song in your heart. Now write your song. It doesn't have to rhyme but it *does* need to be your song.

Objectives

This relaxing visualisation enables clients to look at their identity and uniqueness, becoming aware of where they have come from and where they are going. It may take clients a while to interpret and make their own, perhaps thinking it through and working on it between sessions. Once they have discovered their own unique song, it can help them move on in a positive way.

What's in a name?

Materials needed

Paper, pens.

Instructions

The therapist leads the visualisation:

Get comfortable, relax and close your eyes if you want to.

I invite you to think about your name. (PAUSE) How do you feel when people use your name? (PAUSE) Do you prefer your full name or a shortened version? (PAUSE) Do you have a nickname? (PAUSE) Do you like your nickname? (PAUSE)
Are you happy with your name? (PAUSE) Or would you like to be called something else? (PAUSE) Have you been called names or pet names that you don't like? (PAUSE) What is it like for you when people make a mistake with your name? (PAUSE)
What do you call yourself? (PAUSE) How important to you is your name? (PAUSE)

When you are ready, open your eyes and come back to the here and now. Write down your thoughts and feelings about your name as you became aware of them in the visualisation.

Objectives

The purpose of this visualisation is to focus clients' attention on their name and its significance. Names are important. Encourage clients to realise that they have a choice if they don't wish to be called a particular pet name any more.

Looking at life differently

Materials needed

Paper, pens.

Instructions

The therapist leads the visualisation:

Get comfortable and close your eyes if it helps.

How do you look at life? (PAUSE) Do you see problems and difficulties everywhere? (PAUSE) Or can you sort things out step by step? (PAUSE)
Does life become overwhelming? (PAUSE) With insurmountable problems? (PAUSE) Or do you sleep on it and tackle things in the morning? (PAUSE)
Do you feel unable to cope with all that life throws at you? (PAUSE) Or do you ask for help? (PAUSE) Do you blame other people? (PAUSE) Is it their fault that you are in this mess? (PAUSE) Or do you look at your own responsibility and choices? (PAUSE)
Do you hide and hope it will all go away? (PAUSE) Or do you face up to your own difficulties? (PAUSE)
How would it be if you could look at life differently? (PAUSE) What would your outlook be if you could see some good in the world? (PAUSE)
How would life look if someone came alongside you to support you through your difficulties? (PAUSE) What would you do if you acknowledged that you can't change other people but you can change yourself? (PAUSE)
I invite you to look at life differently. (PAUSE) See how that changes your outlook. (PAUSE)

When you are ready come back to the here and now and open your eyes. Now, write down ways that you could look at life differently.

Objectives

This visualisation could be used when helping a client through depression. It gives clients the opportunity to look at other points of view, not just their existing one. Helping clients to find a positive outlook could be one more step in their moving forward in life's journey.

Shaping the event

Introduction

It is useful to follow a visualisation with an activity using clay. Clay is a natural substance that can be used effectively to express a wide range of emotions. It provides a safe, powerful medium for anger expression. It can bring to the conscious memory messages from the client's unconscious.

Janet West writes: 'Clay has a basic, elemental quality and can be used for messy play as well as for sophisticated symbolic expression. It allows three-dimensional work that can be moulded and altered, thus having more flexibility, sometimes more reality, than painting or drawing' (West, 1992, page 71).

An alternative to natural clay is shop-bought or homemade playdough, with Plasticine as a substitute if all else fails. Clay or its alternative is a tactile substance. Using it can be a very physical experience. It allows the client to express feelings that may not be appropriate outside the therapy room.

The client has permission to bang, pummel, break, reshape, squeeze, mould, model and express the feelings invoked by the visualisation.

If the client is using natural clay, once the object has been created it can be lovingly placed or forcefully thrown outside and will revert back to its origins in the soil.

The mountain climb

Materials needed

Clay, playdough or Plasticine.

Instructions

The therapist leads the visualisation:

Sit comfortably and close your eyes if you want to. Come with me on a mountain climb.

The wind is howling round me. (PAUSE) But I push my way forward up the mountain track. (PAUSE) I am cold. (PAUSE) Buffeted by the wind. (PAUSE) Feeling broken and defeated. (PAUSE) I am drenched to the skin by the torrential rain. (PAUSE)

Many times I slip on the scree. (PAUSE) I fall down the rocky terrain. Each time I pick myself up, determined to carry on. (PAUSE)

I stumble on. (PAUSE) I will not be defeated. (PAUSE) Leaning forward, bracing myself against the wind, I climb upwards. (PAUSE)

After a while of continued slipping and sliding, I allow myself a short rest. (PAUSE) I turn back and am amazed at how far I have climbed. (PAUSE) Even with all the setbacks I have still made progress. (PAUSE)

Then the sun comes out and I find the strength to carry on. (PAUSE)

When you are ready, come back into the room, open your eyes and take a deep breath. Using this clay make a mountain showing the route up it. Now mark your journey on the track showing setbacks and triumphs along the way.

Objectives

This visualisation take the client on a journey. The story is about the troubles in life and how we respond to them. Clients have choices during the visualisation so they are able to make their own story. *The mountain climb* gives clients a chance to reflect on their life so far and to acknowledge and celebrate successes along the way.

The lonely ballerina

Materials needed

Clay, playdough or Plasticine.

Instructions

The therapist leads the visualisation:

This visualisation is about a ballerina. Even if you can't relate to ballet you can take part in it. Make yourself comfortable and close your eyes if you want to.

It's dark inside my little music box. (PAUSE) It's also very squashed. (PAUSE) I lie on my side, with the wooden lid holding me down. (PAUSE) I feel like the lonely ballerina on the music box. (PAUSE)

I hate this. (PAUSE) I've been here for weeks now. (PAUSE) My Owner never seems to open the box and let me dance round in circles. (PAUSE) Maybe she's too old or she has forgotten me. (PAUSE)

I love to dance. (PAUSE) My white ballet dress looks so lovely as I spin round and round on the music box. (PAUSE) The music would play for a while. (PAUSE) I would dance and then my Owner would close the box, pushing me down into the dark. (PAUSE)

I like dancing on the box. (PAUSE) The trouble is, I always feel so dizzy, going around in the same direction, doing exactly the same steps. (PAUSE) When I do this I feel so lonely. (PAUSE) I long to join others in a dance. (PAUSE)

I have an even bigger desire. (PAUSE) If only I could be free of this music box. (PAUSE) I'd love more than anything else to dance my own steps, spin when I want, enjoy movement the way I want it. (PAUSE)

It's no good. My feet are stuck firmly on top of the music box. (PAUSE) I have to dance when my owner opens the music box. There seems just no way out. (PAUSE)

Then something surprising happens. The Owner decides to send the music box to a charity shop. (PAUSE) There all of us unwanted items sit high on a shelf in the back room waiting for someone to price the new stock and put us in the shop. (PAUSE)

One morning a shop assistant reaches up to get the music box and it slips out of his hands. (PAUSE) The music box falls down on the hard tiled floor and smashes to pieces. (PAUSE)

Disaster! (PAUSE)

I open my eyes and look around at the broken pieces on the tiled floor. (PAUSE) I'm feeling in pain and very sorry for myself. (PAUSE)

Then I notice it. My feet have broken away from the music box. (PAUSE) Hesitantly I move my feet, then my legs. (PAUSE) Slowly, carefully, I stand up, checking for broken bones as I do so. Everything seems OK. (PAUSE)

I begin to move in rhythm, slowly at first then faster and faster. (PAUSE) I'm dancing. It's really true. (PAUSE) I can fulfil my dream. (PAUSE) I really can. (PAUSE)

Now I can dance the dance of life. (PAUSE)

OK, when you are ready, open your eyes and come back into the room. Breathe deeply and look around. I would like you to create what you experienced through that visualisation using clay.

Objectives

The Lonely Ballerina paints a scene of a client who is stuck and unable to move forward. As the story progresses, the ballerina realises that she can take control of her life and ownership of her future. This story gives clients a chance to make new decisions in their lives.

Fly away

Materials needed

Clay, playdough or Plasticine.

Instructions

The therapist leads the visualisation:

Make yourself comfortable and close your eyes if you want to. I'm inviting you to fasten your seatbelts ready to go on a flight.

You are at the airfield. (PAUSE) It's a sunny day with little cloud and a slight breeze. (PAUSE) Across the grass you can see your plane waiting. (PAUSE) It's a two-seater Cessna. (PAUSE) The plane looks small and fragile. (PAUSE) What are you thinking? How are you feeling? (PAUSE)

Are you looking forward to going up in the sky to fly like a bird? (PAUSE) Or are you frightened of heights? (PAUSE) Wondering if the plane is strong enough and powerful enough to keep you safe? (PAUSE)

The pilot arrives. (PAUSE) He checks the engine for fuel and does a visual inspection of the plane's exterior. (PAUSE) You both climb in the cockpit. (PAUSE) You fasten your seatbelt. (PAUSE) Then you put on headphones. (PAUSE)

The pilot goes through his checks. (PAUSE) He speaks to the control tower and starts his engine. (PAUSE) Then he taxies on to the runway. (PAUSE)

You realise there is no turning back now. (PAUSE) You are filled with strong emotions. (PAUSE) What emotions are you experiencing? (PAUSE) What are you thinking? (PAUSE)

In front of you is a long strip of tarmac. (PAUSE) The pilot accelerates. (PAUSE) The noise is deafening and you are glad of your headphones. (PAUSE) The plane goes faster and faster along to runway. (PAUSE) Then with a bump the little plane goes up into the air, climbing high above the houses. (PAUSE) How do you feel? (PAUSE) Exhilarated? (PAUSE) Terrified? (PAUSE)

The plane flies over the countryside. (PAUSE) The propeller in front of you is turning so fast it appears to be standing still. (PAUSE) What's that like? (PAUSE) You can see cars and houses like toys way below. (PAUSE)

Occasionally the plane is buffeted by a gust of wind. (PAUSE) You are tipping from side to side. (PAUSE) How do you feel? (PAUSE) Can you trust the pilot to keep you safe? (PAUSE)

The engine is very noisy. You almost have to shout through your microphone to talk to the pilot. (PAUSE) Yet there is a feeling of stillness and beauty as you rise above the landscape below. (PAUSE)

The plane continues its flight. (PAUSE) As you look down at the view below you decide to leave your problems behind and enjoy the journey. (PAUSE)

The plane turns back to return to the airfield. (PAUSE) You hear the control tower giving the OK for landing. (PAUSE) The strip of tarmac comes into view. (PAUSE) It almost seems as if the plane will crash down on it. (PAUSE) The pilot brings the nose up at the last moment and you land with a bump. (PAUSE) The plane taxies along the runway, slowing down, then turning to park. (PAUSE)

How do you feel now? (PAUSE) Was that a pleasure trip? (PAUSE) The plane has stopped. (PAUSE) The pilot has turned the engine off. (PAUSE) Silence. (PAUSE)

When you are ready, take off your headphones, undo your seatbelt, open the door, climb out of the plane and come back to the here and now with your eyes open.

Now, using the clay make a model of your experience during the visualisation.

Objectives

The flight in a light aircraft takes clients through a range of emotions. All the way through the visualisation clients make choices for themselves. This gives them control of how their own story develops. Clients can experience different emotions throughout the flight. They are encouraged to acknowledge their own thoughts and feelings.

Burning rubber

Materials needed

Clay, playdough or Plasticine.

Instructions

The therapist leads the visualisation:

Get comfortable, close your eyes if you want to, put on your helmet. You are about to go on a motorbike ride.

What kind of motorbike are you on? (PAUSE) A Norton? (PAUSE) A Honda Goldwing? (PAUSE) A BMW? (PAUSE) A Harley-Davidson? (PAUSE) Or something smaller? (PAUSE) Perhaps little more than a motorised pushbike? (PAUSE)

Where are you going? (PAUSE) On holiday? (PAUSE) Home from work? (PAUSE) Riding into the city? (PAUSE) Or are you delivering pizzas? (PAUSE)

Are you the motorbike driver? (PAUSE) Or riding pillion at the back? (PAUSE)

How do you feel? (PAUSE) Is the motorbike going fast and recklessly? (PAUSE) Or carefully and with consideration? (PAUSE)

The wind is rushing noisily past you, buffeting your helmet. (PAUSE) Is this an adventure? (PAUSE) Or a nightmare? (PAUSE)

You travel on and on. (PAUSE) Leaning into the bends. (PAUSE) Do you feel at one with your machine? (PAUSE) Or do you feel vulnerable and scared? (PAUSE)

The motorbike turns into the car park. (PAUSE) You climb off and remove your helmet. (PAUSE)

When you are ready, open your eyes and come back to the here and now. I invite you using some clay to model your experience of the motorbike ride.

Objectives

In this visualisation the client experiences a motorbike journey. Is this true adventure or a scary nightmare? Each client will have his or her own interpretation of the story. During the visualisation clients are making decisions and owning their feelings.

The prison cell

Materials needed

Clay, playdough or Plasticine.

Instructions

The therapist leads the visualisation:

Get into a comfortable position and close your eyes if you want to. We are going on a journey to a rather uncomfortable place – a prison cell.

Look around your prison cell. (PAUSE) What do you see? What is in your prison cell? (PAUSE) What are the walls like? (PAUSE) Rough? Decorated? (PAUSE) Painted? (PAUSE) Plain? (PAUSE)
    What else is in your cell? (PAUSE) A bed? (PAUSE) A chair? (PAUSE) A small table? (PAUSE) Anything else? (PAUSE)
    What are the other prisoners like? (PAUSE) Friendly? (PAUSE) Hostile? (PAUSE) Gentle? (PAUSE) Violent? (PAUSE)
    What is the food like? (PAUSE) Tasty and nutritious? (PAUSE) Horrible and bad for you? (PAUSE) Do you get tea and coffee? (PAUSE) Or just cold water? (PAUSE)
    Look at the window. (PAUSE) What are bars like? (PAUSE) How much can you see outside with window? (PAUSE) Is it pleasant and green? Or ugly and grey? (PAUSE)
    Now turn towards the door. (PAUSE) You notice for the first time that the door is wide open. (PAUSE) You are free to leave the prison cell. (PAUSE) What will you decide to do? (PAUSE) Will you leave your cell for ever? (PAUSE) Or will you stay there? (PAUSE) It's your choice. (PAUSE)

When you are ready come back in the room and open your eyes. Using the clay, model your thoughts, feelings and actions around the cell and whether you will stay in it or not.

Objectives

The prison cell is a visualisation about freedom. The character in the story thinks and feels as if he or she is still a prisoner. Many clients will empathise with this and reflect on their own lives. The door is open and the prisoner is free to leave. Will the client move into this freedom, or will he or she stay with the familiar in the prison cell?

A wedding

Materials needed

Clay, playdough or Plasticine.

Instructions

The therapist leads the visualisation:

Make yourself comfortable and close your eyes if you wish. I invite you to come to the wedding.

You are well dressed and look elegant and enchanting. (PAUSE) How are you feeling inside? (PAUSE) Are your clothes just a mask? (PAUSE) What are you thinking? (PAUSE)
What is your role in the wedding? (PAUSE) Bridesmaid? (PAUSE) Best man? (PAUSE) Mother? (PAUSE) Father? (PAUSE) Cousin? (PAUSE) Friend? (PAUSE) Old flame? (PAUSE)
Do you hope to meet people at the wedding? (PAUSE) Old friends? (PAUSE) New love? (PAUSE)
In the church, where are sitting? (PAUSE) On the bride's side? (PAUSE) Or on the groom's side? (PAUSE) How do you feel? (PAUSE) Are you comfortable being in a church? (PAUSE)
The service starts. (PAUSE) Vows are said. (PAUSE) And, before you know it, Mr and Mrs . . . process down the aisle. (PAUSE)
The congregation pour out into the sunshine. (PAUSE) People are commenting: 'Such lovely weather for a wedding.' (PAUSE) 'Doesn't the bride look beautiful?' (PAUSE) 'What cute little bridesmaids!' (PAUSE)
How do you feel? (PAUSE) Are you involved and genuinely pleased for the happy couple? (PAUSE) Or do you experience pain? (PAUSE) Or do you yearn for a love lost or a love not yet found? (PAUSE)

Throw a handful of confetti over the happy couple, open your eyes and come back into the room. Now, using clay, make a shape to express your feelings about this visualisation.

Objectives

A wedding is often a poignant event, evoking strong emotions in clients. This visualisation takes clients through the story, looking at the wedding from different angles. Clients are given the opportunity to look into their thoughts and feelings surrounding a wedding. They may also make a new script decision about the way forward in their lives.

Uncharted waters

Materials needed

Clay, playdough or Plasticine.

Instructions

The therapist leads the visualisation:

Get comfortable and close your eyes if you want to.

Imagine you are going on a long journey by ship. (PAUSE) The weather is stormy. (PAUSE) The seas are treacherous. (PAUSE) Only the bravest of sailors attempt this route. (PAUSE) You are tired, worn down and almost defeated. (PAUSE)

A cry goes up. (PAUSE) There is land ahead. (PAUSE) How do you feel? (PAUSE) What do you think as you take your binoculars and scan the horizon? (PAUSE)

Land is in sight. (PAUSE) But the journey is not over. (PAUSE) There are many hidden rocks. (PAUSE) And the waters must be navigated with care and skill. (PAUSE)

The ship is anchored in the bay. (PAUSE) Calm. (PAUSE) Stillness. (PAUSE) The only sound is the gentle lap of the waves against the hull of the ship. (PAUSE)

You go ashore in a small rowing-boat. (PAUSE) How do you feel? (PAUSE) Are you longing to set foot on land? (PAUSE)

As you step out of the small boat you feel weighed down. (PAUSE) All the trouble and anxiety of the journey is clinging to you. (PAUSE) You wonder what to do. (PAUSE) Is it possible to get rid of these feelings of trouble and anxiety? (PAUSE)

Then you have a plan. (PAUSE) You walk inland and find a clearing in the woods. (PAUSE) You dig a deep hole. (PAUSE) You throw all the trouble and anxiety you have into the hole. (PAUSE) Then you draw a map of where the hole is. (PAUSE)

With a lighter step you walk back through the woods to the beach. (PAUSE) It is time for the ship to sail. (PAUSE) You climb into the rowing-boat and back into the ship. (PAUSE)

On the journey home you discover you still have the map that shows where you left your trouble and anxiety. (PAUSE) What will you do? (PAUSE) Throw it overboard? (PAUSE) Burn it? (PAUSE) Tear it up? (PAUSE) Or keep it so you can return and dig up your trouble and anxiety later? (PAUSE)

Take a deep breath and come back to the here and now, opening your eyes. Using clay, recreate the hole in which you can throw your trouble and anxiety. Throw them in and press more clay on the top. Then squash the ball of clay, destroying those negative feelings.

Objectives

This nautical visualisation is about life and all its difficulties. The client is taken through hazards at sea and makes decisions as the story progresses. Towards the end the person in the scenario puts his or her troubles in a deep hole. The client is left with the decision about whether to keep the map of the buried troubles or to destroy it. We all have difficulties in life, and this visualisation encourages the client to move on and leave the past behind.

Cliff walk

Materials needed

Clay, playdough or Plasticine.

Instructions

The therapist leads the visualisation:

Get comfortable, close your eyes if you want to and get ready for a walk in your imagination.

Start by visualising a high cliff, with the sea crashing on the rocks below. (PAUSE) Feel the wind in your face. (PAUSE) Smell the salt in the spray. (PAUSE) Listen to the gulls as they wheel and call above you. (PAUSE) Look at the sea sparkling along the coast. (PAUSE)
    You climb steadily upwards. (PAUSE) You reach the top of the headland. (PAUSE) You walk along the cliff path, enjoying the experience. (PAUSE) Look in the distance to the next bay. (PAUSE) As you walk you are aware of the beauty of this awesome place. (PAUSE)
    Breathe deeply and enjoy the view. (PAUSE) Look back and see how far you have climbed. (PAUSE) Rest for a while in this fabulous place. (PAUSE)
    Leave the stresses of everyday life behind. (PAUSE) Feel the sun on your back. (PAUSE) Enjoy the pleasure of being out of doors in a beautiful place. (PAUSE) Allow yourself to feel refreshed and invigorated. (PAUSE)

I invite you to come back down the cliff path. When you are ready, open your eyes and come back to this room. Using the clay we have here make something to represent your experience of going on the cliff walk.

Objectives

This is a visualisation aimed at clients who need to relax. The story involves a walk along a cliff path, with sensory stimulation (sights, sounds, smells) for clients to experience in their imagination. They can leave the stresses of everyday life behind and move forward into a more relaxed existence.

Moving through

Introduction

Visualisation accompanying or followed by movement can be an expression of the heart. The client may feel able to show through movement what he or she cannot say in words.

Movement can include dance, which can symbolise deep feelings. Dance has many different forms, giving the client varied avenues for expression. This can help clients gain insight into themselves.

Dance as a therapy began in 1942 with the work of Marian Chase. It eventually became known as 'dance movement therapy'. It is based on the principle that movement reflects a person's thinking and feeling and can result in a sense of renewal, unity and completeness.

Emotional changes can occur when the therapist encourages exploring new movement patterns. These movements are based on movement principles developed by Rudolph Laban (1879-1958). These include:

❐ Body in action – whole body, body parts, joints moving, surfaces in contact.

❐ Body shape – symmetry, asymmetry, wide/open, curved, twisted.

❐ Body flow – successive, simultaneous, bound, free, sustained, impulsive.

❐ Action in body – jumping, turning, twisting, gesturing, stillness.

❐ Action in space – rising, sinking, gathering, scattering, advancing, retreating.

- ☐ Dimensions of space – personal, high, middle, deep, up, down, in front, behind, to the left, to the right.

- ☐ Dynamics – direct pathways, indirect pathways.

- ☐ Time – fast. slow, rhythmic, arrhythmic.

- ☐ Phrasing – long, short, accented.

- ☐ Quality – mood.

- ☐ Relationships – solo, duo, group.

- ☐ Proximity – near, far.

- ☐ Contact – touch, weight bearing, supporting.

Reaching towards the sun

Materials needed

None, though scarves and streamers can enhance the effect of movement.

Instructions

The therapist leads the visualisation:

This is a visualisation involving physical movement. You can do it with your eyes shut, if you want. Get into position, crouched on the floor ready to begin.

It's night time and the storm is blowing the sunflower stalk so far over that it is almost on the ground. (PAUSE) Again and again the sunflower is blown, sometimes one way and sometimes the other way. (PAUSE) The beautiful flower is being battered and bruised. (PAUSE) It is covered in rain. (PAUSE) It is painful to be in such a fierce storm. (PAUSE)
There is a tiny bit of light at the very bottom of the sky. (PAUSE) The sunflower, still battered and bruised and covered in rain, looks longingly towards it. (PAUSE) If only the sun would rise. (PAUSE)
The light in the sky becomes brighter, piercing the gloom of the night. Black turns to grey and then the hint of blue. (PAUSE) Suddenly, the top of the sun appears just above the horizon, its beams pushing the darkness fully away. (PAUSE) The sunflower, still bruised, battered and very wet, watches in eager anticipation of the sun's full light. (PAUSE)
Quite quickly the sun rises above the horizon, its beams shining on the sunflower. (PAUSE) In response, the bedraggled sunflower starts to open its petals to the sun's full light. (PAUSE)
The sun rises further in the sky and the raindrops on the sunflower slowly evaporate. (PAUSE) As the sun moves

across the sky, the sunflower follows it, always with its face towards the sun. (PAUSE) It is as if the sunflower is smiling. (PAUSE)

Days go by and each morning the battered sunflower follows the sun as it moves across the sky. (PAUSE) Slowly, almost imperceptibly, the damage of the storm starts to repair itself. The bruises are healing and the disfigured petals caused by the battering start to straighten out. (PAUSE) The healing has begun. (PAUSE)

The bruising and battering of the night's storm are becoming a distant memory. (PAUSE) The sunflower is enjoying the warmth and full power of the sun's rays. (PAUSE)

It's a new day. (PAUSE)

Now, when you are ready, become yourself again, perhaps turning around once to leave behind the sunflower visualisation you have portrayed, and return to the room.

Objectives

This visualisation could be used for working with survivors. It is the story of a sunflower, bruised and battered by the storm. The sunflower turns towards the sun and slowly finds healing and strength. This movement activity encourages clients to reach out for health and strength and to see it as a new day.

Rising on eagle's wings

Materials needed

None, though scarves and streamers can enhance the effect of movement.

Instructions

The therapist leads the visualisation:

In this visualisation I invite you to imagine yourself as an eagle flying, moving around as the visualisation progresses. Start by finding somewhere you can move safety. Close your eyes if you want to. Let's begin.

The eagle is perched on the branch of a tree, watching the other birds flying around. (PAUSE) Be aware of the eagle's feelings about being stuck in the tree. (PAUSE) Now, with some effort, the eagle starts to flex its wings. Be aware of the effort involved. (PAUSE) The eagle starts to rise, then descends with disappointment. (PAUSE) It tries again. Notice how difficult it is.
    Then the eagle returns to its branch. (PAUSE) It remembers that this was the pattern many times when it was still in the nest, practicing to strengthen its wings. (PAUSE) Finally, with one supreme effort, the eagle tries again, flapping its wings rapidly. (PAUSE) This time the eagle catches the breeze and begins to fly. It is hard work, but worth it. (PAUSE)
    The eagle reaches the bottom of the mountain, where there is a thermal rising upwards. (PAUSE) Suddenly, it catches the thermal and begins to rise up, floating in circles with wings spread wide. (PAUSE) Higher and higher the eagle travels, making slight adjustments with its wings to keep in the thermal. (PAUSE) Be aware of how much more the eagle can see from this perspective. (PAUSE)
    Now the eagle is near the top of the mountain. (PAUSE) It notices a rocky crag at the top of a high

cliff. *(PAUSE)* With slight adjustment of its wings it effortlessly moves to the crag and lands. *(PAUSE)* Be aware of the wind blowing through the eagle's feathers. *(PAUSE)* Feel the strength of the eagle as it holds firmly to its perch high up on the cliff. *(PAUSE)*

See what the eagle sees. *(PAUSE)* The fabulous perspective. *(PAUSE)* The other mountains in the distance. *(PAUSE)* See down below how high the eagle has risen. *(PAUSE)* No more is it confined to a tree near ground level. *(PAUSE)* All the difficulties the eagle faced have been left far below. *(PAUSE)* From this elevation everything looks very different. *(PAUSE)* Enjoy it. *(PAUSE)* Savour it. *(PAUSE)* Embrace the eagle's perspective. *(PAUSE)*

When you are ready come to land in this room, open your eyes and come back to ground level.

Objectives

This visualisation is about rising above one's problems. It shows the struggle of the eagle to start flying and to catch the thermal. It is easy to look at other people and see them 'soaring', not realising the struggle and the healing process that has so often gone before.

The littlest dolphin

Materials needed

None, though scarves and streamers can enhance the effect of movement.

Instructions

The therapist leads the visualisation:

This is a therapeutic story involving movement. Find a place where you can move around safely, close your eyes if you want to and become the main character in the story.

I'm the littlest dolphin in the ocean. (PAUSE) When everyone else is coming up for air, I'm the one who always gets left behind. (PAUSE) Sometimes I worry that I won't reach the light at the surface and will end up drowning without any fresh air in my lungs. (PAUSE)

You see, my tail doesn't work as well as it should. (PAUSE) I had an accident soon after I was born. I was little and helpless and one of the big dolphins – I think it was a grown male – wooshed past me and hit my tail hard, breaking a couple of bones. (PAUSE)

It healed up but it's never worked properly since. (PAUSE) My body is sleek and strong but my tail just doesn't keep me going fast enough. (PAUSE)

I really need this air. (PAUSE) I can see the light up above me. (PAUSE) My mum and my big sister are almost there but I just can't seem to make it. (PAUSE)

I feel so, so tired. (PAUSE) I want to give up and just sink back down into the dark ocean below me. Maybe I just won't bother . . . (PAUSE)

What's that? My sister's calling me. 'You can make it, Littlest Dolphin. You can do it. Only a few more wiggles of your tail and fins and you'll be there.' (PAUSE)

'No, it's no good. I'm just too tired.' (PAUSE)

'Don't give up, little one, don't give up.' It's my mum calling to me. *(PAUSE)* She continues: 'My nose is just about to break the surface. You can make it, too.' *(PAUSE)*

Hope is rising in me. Maybe they're right. *(PAUSE)* Yes, I think I can make it. *(PAUSE)* One more flick of my tail, two, three. *(PAUSE)* But it's so hard and my lungs are ready to burst. *(PAUSE)*

'Come on, little one, come on,' cry my mum and sister in unison, peeking at me with their heads just below the surface. *(PAUSE)*

Suddenly, my nose feels the cold, welcoming air. *(PAUSE)* I release that staleness from my lungs and breathe in the fresh, cold air of the surface. *(PAUSE)*

I'm gasping with the effort I put in. *(PAUSE)* But I'm so, so happy that my struggle was rewarded and I got here. *(PAUSE)* It was all worth it. *(PAUSE)*

When you're ready, float back into this room and open your eyes. Feel your feet firmly on the floor and return to the here and now.

Objectives

The Littlest Dolphin is a therapeutic story about a dolphin struggling but not giving up. The story shows the importance of support and encouragement from others. Listening to this story can give clients strength to carry on.

A growing child

Materials needed

None.

Instructions

The therapist leads the visualisation:

In this visualisation I invite you to take part in a series of movements as the story progresses. Start by lying on the floor looking upwards, arms by your sides.

Imagine you are a newborn baby. (PAUSE) You are not able to move your head from side to side yet. You blink only occasionally. (PAUSE) Be aware of how restricted it feels. (PAUSE)

Now you are a little older. You can move your head from side to side. (PAUSE) Note how much more you can see. (PAUSE)

You begin to explore your hands. (PAUSE) They come into your field of vision and you look at them and their movements with curiosity. (PAUSE)

You have reached a major milestone. You can turn over. (PAUSE) Turn on to your tummy and support the front part of your body with your arms. (PAUSE) Notice how much more you can see. (PAUSE)

You begin to move, crawling along. (PAUSE) Be aware of what a difference this makes to you. (PAUSE)

You can sit on your own. (PAUSE) Look around and notice how much more you can see. (PAUSE)

With some effort you get to your feet and begin, slowly and hesitantly, to walk around. (PAUSE) See what that is like. (PAUSE)

OK, turn round once, leave your babyhood behind you and return to the here and now in this room.

Objectives

This visualisation, involving movement, can help clients connect with the child they once were. It allows clients to experience what it is like to be helpless, and to develop and move on to maturity. The activity often helps people to gain insight in a profound way.

Swimming with dolphins

Materials needed

None, though scarves and streamers can enhance the effect of movement.

Instructions

The therapist leads the visualisation:

When you are comfortable with your eyes closed we will begin.

You are going to swim with dolphins. (PAUSE) How do you feel? (PAUSE) Excited? (PAUSE) Scared? (PAUSE) What are you thinking? (PAUSE) Dangerous? (PAUSE) Thrilling? (PAUSE)
  Is this an opportunity of a lifetime for you? (PAUSE)
  Where are you? (PAUSE) Are you in your own country? (PAUSE) Or another country? (PAUSE)
  Are you in a sheltered environment? (PAUSE) Are people there to guide and keep you safe? (PAUSE) Are you in a boat at sea, where wild dolphins have come alongside? (PAUSE)
  You get in the water to swim with the dolphins. (PAUSE) How do you feel? (PAUSE) What are you thinking? (PAUSE)
  The dolphins come towards you. (PAUSE) What do you do? (PAUSE) Keep still? (PAUSE) Move towards them? (PAUSE) Freeze? (PAUSE)
  The dolphins let you touch them. (PAUSE) They seem to be smiling. (PAUSE) How do you feel? (PAUSE)
  You linger a while, watching as they swim curiously around you. (PAUSE)
  It's time to leave. (PAUSE) With one last touch you say goodbye to the dolphins. (PAUSE)

Come out of the water, open your eyes and back to the here and now. Recreate the experience of swimming with dolphins using dance and movement.

Objectives

The aim of *Swimming with Dolphins* is to get clients to experience a range of feelings and thinking in a way that is relatively safe. Each client will have a different reaction to this visualisation and subsequent activity.

Race of life

Materials needed

None, though scarves and streamers can enhance the effect of movement.

Instructions

The therapist leads the visualisation:

Find a comfortable position, relax and close your eyes if you want to.

I want you to imagine that you are running in a cross-country race. (PAUSE) You have been practising for over a year. (PAUSE) You have the right clothing. (PAUSE) You have been on a special diet. (PAUSE) You have broken in your running shoes. (PAUSE) You are ready. (PAUSE) How do you feel? (PAUSE) What are you thinking? (PAUSE)

The race begins. (PAUSE) You jog along the track in a large crowd. (PAUSE) Gradually you settle down and find your pace. (PAUSE) The runners spread out. (PAUSE) It is quieter now. (PAUSE)

The track becomes a footpath. (PAUSE) It turns up a hill. (PAUSE) And into the woods. (PAUSE)

It is darker and cooler now. (PAUSE) You continue for several miles, winding along the forest tracks. (PAUSE) Occasionally you stumble. (PAUSE) How do you feel? (PAUSE) Are you alone? (PAUSE) Or running with a friend? (PAUSE) Are at the front? (PAUSE) The middle? (PAUSE) Or at the back? (PAUSE)

Your journey progresses across muddy fields. (PAUSE) You are beginning to feel the strain. (PAUSE) Do you want to give up? (PAUSE) Or are you determined to break through the pain barrier? (PAUSE)

You are struggling. (PAUSE) Then you see a drinks station ahead. (PAUSE) How do you feel? (PAUSE)

You take a drink. (PAUSE) Refreshed, you think you have the strength to carry on. (PAUSE)

The spectators come into view. (PAUSE) Your feet are hurting. (PAUSE) Your legs are tired. (PAUSE) The finishing line is just in sight. (PAUSE)

A final push and you make it. (PAUSE) You have finished the race. (PAUSE) What is that like? (PAUSE)

Now go and receive your ribboned medal. (PAUSE)

When you are ready, come back into the here and now and open your eyes. Now, using your body do a series of movements to show your progress and achievement throughout the race.

Objectives

This visualisation goes through the highs and lows of life leading to success. The race in the story shows clients the reality of life and the fact that they *will* face problems from time to time. Determination will enable them to face each difficulty, one step at a time.

In touch with your body

Materials needed

None.

Instructions

The therapist leads the visualisation:

Get comfortable and close your eyes if you want to.

I invite you to breathe deeply and relax. (PAUSE) be aware of your whole body. (PAUSE) How does it feel? (PAUSE) Are you anxious? (PAUSE) Tense? (PAUSE) Do you have any aches or pains? (PAUSE)

I want you to focus on your feet. (PAUSE) Wriggle your toes. (PAUSE) Stretch your ankles. (PAUSE) Now relax your feet. (PAUSE) Now tense and relax your leg muscles. (PAUSE)

Think about the trunk area of your body. (PAUSE) Be aware of your breathing. (PAUSE) Relax your abdomen. (PAUSE) Relax your rib cage. (PAUSE) Put your hand on your chest and feel your ribs go up and down as you breathe. (PAUSE)

Tense and relax your arm muscles. (PAUSE) Let your shoulders tense up and then relax and go down. (PAUSE) Tense and relax your neck and facial muscles. (PAUSE)

Be aware of what is going on with your body. (PAUSE) Can you sense the blood pumping around? (PAUSE) Can you feel your pulse? (PAUSE)

Think about how complex our bodies are. (PAUSE) Everything working in harmony to keep us healthy. (PAUSE)

Breathe deeply and when you are ready come back to the here and now.

Objectives

This is a form of gentle relaxation. It encourages clients to think about their bodies, learning how to relax effectively. The eventual aim is to encourage them to relax regularly, taking care of their bodies.

Wild swimming

Materials needed

None, though scarves and streamers can enhance the effect of movement.

Instructions

The therapist leads the visualisation:

Make sure you are comfortable and close your eyes if you want to.

You are going for a swim. (PAUSE) You are at a large lake with mountains in the distance. (PAUSE) The air is almost still. (PAUSE) Only a gentle breeze is disturbing the surface of the water. (PAUSE) The sky is blue and almost cloudless. (PAUSE) the sun is shining. (PAUSE) The weather is pleasantly warm. (PAUSE)

You leave your bag of clothes on the stony beach. (PAUSE) Now walk down to the water's edge. (PAUSE) You are wearing beach shoes so you don't hurt your feet. (PAUSE) As you walk, be aware of your surroundings. (PAUSE) What can you see? (PAUSE) What can you hear? (PAUSE) How do you feel? (PAUSE) What are you thinking? (PAUSE)

You enter the water. (PAUSE) It is cool and refreshing. (PAUSE) You wade in until it is deep enough to swim. (PAUSE) Now lean forward and swim. (PAUSE) Enjoy the feeling of the water over your body. (PAUSE)

You swim strongly along the lakeside. (PAUSE) Enjoy the sight of the trees as you go. (PAUSE) There is a strong smell of pine from the forest around the lake. (PAUSE)

Now relax. (PAUSE) You float on your back and enjoy looking at the sky. (PAUSE) You watch birds fly high above you. (PAUSE) Breathe deeply and enjoy the peace and tranquillity. (PAUSE)

You stand up and look into the water. (PAUSE) It is crystal clear. (PAUSE) And you can see little fish swimming around your legs. (PAUSE)

You wade back to the shore feeling cool and refreshed. (PAUSE)

Reach for your towel, dry yourself off and come back to the here and now, opening your eyes. Now use your body to show in movement the relaxation you have enjoyed while swimming in the lake.

Objectives

This visualisation is a powerful relaxation. It encourages clients to enter into the story and experience the atmosphere and enjoyment of swimming in the wild. Be aware that clients who can't swim may find this activity a source of fear and tension instead!

Bringing colour to the story

Introduction

Painting using colours with visualisation need not be an anxious experience. The therapist can reassure clients that they are painting for themselves and not for display to others. There is no set standard to which they need to attain.

Painting can be a relaxed, thoughtful activity. Clients have permission to apply colours to the paper in any way they want. Of course, it is important that they also respect the room and take care not to damage its furniture and fittings. With children and with some enthusiastic adults it is advisable to have clear ground rules about the use of paints.

There is a wide choice of types of paint, from oils to watercolours to expensive acrylics. Most therapists who have paint available will use poster paints (the kind used in schools) because they are water-based and the brushes are easy to clean. It is also useful to have some oil pastels.

Using paint can be seen as a form of self-healing, a means of expression of the emotions where the process is more important than what is produced. It is vital for the therapist to accept what is painted without criticism, evaluation or interpretation.

Some clients may find finger- or hand-painting more effective than using a brush because it provides freedom to make a mess. There is also something very sensory based in using fingers and hands rather than the impersonal medium of a brush. Consider having poster paint and small pots (such as yoghurt pots) available for this. Alternatively, it is possible to buy from craft and toy shops finger-paints that have been thickened for ease of use.

Another aspect to consider is colour. The colours used by the client may have symbolic significance. Be aware, though, of colour therapy approaches where green always means one thing (usually freshness, new life) and red always means anger or danger. Colours can mean different things to different people according to the person's culture and family background. If a therapist wants to know what a particular colour symbolises, simply ask the client.

The cloud

Materials needed

Paints, pastels, brushes, paper.

Instructions

The therapist leads the visualisation:

Get comfortable, close your eyes and prepare for this visualisation.

I used to live in a cloud. (PAUSE) It was dark. (PAUSE) Frightening. (PAUSE) Lonely. (PAUSE) I felt so alone and helpless. (PAUSE)

Then things changed in my life. (PAUSE) And for a while I felt I had escaped from the cloud. But sometimes at night I would be covered with a cloud of panic. (PAUSE) What if my nightmare starts again? (PAUSE)

Years have passed and you would think I would have got over it by now. (PAUSE) Nobody knows the torment I suffer when the cloud descends. (PAUSE) It can come on suddenly: a song, a phrase, an incident at work . . . (PAUSE)

I like to think I've forgiven the adults for not protecting me, and the people who caused my pain. (PAUSE) Oh, how many times I've had to forgive them so that I could escape from this cloud, my prison. (PAUSE)

It's an uphill journey but I will be free. (PAUSE) Because I am a survivor. (PAUSE)

Think about the cloud. Depict it on paper using paint, colour and texture. When you have finished look at the picture and think of some positive ways in which you have learned to cope. Put these positives on to the paper using words or colours.

Now look at your work. You are a survivor!

Objectives

This is an activity specifically for survivors of abuse, whether as a child or an adult. The visualisation is about moving on. The story talks about recurring memories or difficulties. It then progresses towards freedom from the past. The aim is to help survivors recognise what they are going through and to celebrate their progress so far.

Colours of anxiety

Materials needed

Paints, pastels, brushes, paper.

Instructions

The therapist leads the visualisation:

Close your eyes if you want to and get comfortable.

Running. Hurrying. Rushing. (PAUSE) Stumbling. Checking. Falling. (PAUSE) Failing. Panicking. Anxious. (PAUSE) Out of control. Overwhelmed. Defeated. (PAUSE)
    How did I get here? (PAUSE) How can I escape this dark and terrifying place? (PAUSE)
    I pick myself up. (PAUSE) Am I OK? (PAUSE)
    Breathing. (PAUSE)
Heart. (PAUSE) Body. (PAUSE) Limbs. (PAUSE)
    Find a safe place. (PAUSE) A place where I can think. (PAUSE) Be myself. (PAUSE) Take stock of the situation. (PAUSE)
    Take time for me. (PAUSE) Relax. (PAUSE) Breathe. (PAUSE) Think. (PAUSE) Observe. (PAUSE)
    Go out. (PAUSE) Go on. (PAUSE) Continue. (PAUSE) Break through. (PAUSE) Break out. (PAUSE)
    Achieve. (PAUSE) Succeed. (PAUSE) LIVE! (PAUSE)

Get your client to express his or her anxiety on paper using paints to create the colours of anxiety. On a separate piece of paper the client then writes positive words to counteract the anxiety. These are then cut out and placed on the picture. The client can use his or her words or you could provide words and phrases from the visualisation such as: Take time for me. Relax. Breathe. Think. Observe. Go out. Go on. Continue. Break through. Break out. Achieve. Succeed. LIVE!

Objectives

People with anxiety are often overwhelmed with feelings. This visualisation, and its associated activity, enables clients to explore the feelings involved. The objective is to help clients understand what exactly are their feelings leading to anxiety and so are better able to deal with them. Using colour to identify them can help clients understand their feelings and learn to take control of them.

I'm a survivor

Materials needed

Paints, pastels, brushes, paper.

Instructions

The therapist leads the visualisation:

Get comfortable and close your eyes if you want to. Listen to these words and let them speak to you.

Struggle. (PAUSE) Pain. (PAUSE) Defeat. (PAUSE) Battered. (PAUSE) Bruised. (PAUSE)
    Lonely. (PAUSE) Crying. (PAUSE) Cold. (PAUSE) Misunderstood. (PAUSE) Unwanted. (PAUSE)
    Needy. (PAUSE) Stressed. (PAUSE) Negative. (PAUSE) Friendless. (PAUSE) Uncared for. (PAUSE) Lost. (PAUSE)
    Determined. (PAUSE) Positive. (PAUSE) Facing the truth. (PAUSE) Expressing myself. (PAUSE) Reaching out to others. (PAUSE) Caring for me. (PAUSE)
    Recognising my needs. (PAUSE) And not just recognising my needs but doing something to protect and care for myself. (PAUSE)
    I will not be intimidated. (PAUSE) Bullied. (PAUSE) Or abused. (PAUSE) I will nurture myself and others. (PAUSE)
    I am a survivor. (PAUSE)

When you are ready, breathe deeply, open your eyes and come back into the room. Using the paints or pastels create a picture of how you feel and think right now.

Objectives

This is a visualisation aimed particularly at survivors. It emphasises self-worth and underlines the importance of self-care. It encourages clients to become determined, using all their resources to carry on and succeed in life.

The colour of music

Materials needed

Paints, pastels, brushes, paper.

Instructions

The therapist leads the visualisation:

In this visualisation I invite you to become a musical instrument. Get yourself comfortable, close your eyes if you want and we can begin.

Imagine yourself as a musical instrument. (PAUSE) What kind of instrument are you? (PAUSE) Classical? (PAUSE) Modern? (PAUSE) Quiet? (PAUSE) Loud? (PAUSE)
    What about your appearance? (PAUSE) Are you carefully made by a crafts person? (PAUSE) Or mass produced in a factory? (PAUSE) Are you shiny? (PAUSE) Attractive? (PAUSE) Dull? (PAUSE) Ugly? (PAUSE) Are you big? (PAUSE) Or small? (PAUSE)
    Think of the sound you make. (PAUSE) Is it beautiful? (PAUSE) Smooth? (PAUSE) Clashing? (PAUSE) In harmony? (PAUSE) Out of harmony? (PAUSE) In tune? (PAUSE) Or out of tune? (PAUSE)
    Now think of yourself in relation to other musical instruments. (PAUSE) Are you a soloist? (PAUSE) In harmony? (PAUSE) In competition? Blending in? (PAUSE) Standing out? (PAUSE) Or, like the tinkling triangle, the last instrument to be noticed? (PAUSE)

When you are ready, open your eyes and come back to sitting in this room. I would now like you to use paint to show the colours of the music you created as a musical instrument. Show all the colours you want. Use your intuition rather than just your thinking.

Objectives

The objective of this visualisation is to give clients the knowledge of who they are. The story enables clients to find where they fit in. The activity promotes self-awareness and relationship with others.

Volcanic eruption

Materials needed

Paints, pastels, brushes, paper.

Instructions

The therapist leads the visualisation:

Make yourself comfortable and close your eyes if you would like.

Imagine you are watching a volcano erupting. (PAUSE) A loud explosion. (PAUSE) Smoke fills the sky. (PAUSE) Lava and rocks spew out from the mouth of the volcano. (PAUSE)

Heat. (PAUSE) Fire. (PAUSE) Danger. (PAUSE) Devastation. (PAUSE) On and on the lava pours down the mountain. (PAUSE) Uprooting trees. (PAUSE) Hurling rocks into the valley below. (PAUSE)

See the power of nature. (PAUSE) The changing landscape. (PAUSE) The destruction. (PAUSE)

How do you feel? (PAUSE) Can you smell the sulphurous gas? (PAUSE) Can you hear the crashing, breaking, destruction as everything in the way is engulfed? (PAUSE)

What do you see? (PAUSE) What are you thinking? (PAUSE) Are you in danger? (PAUSE) Or are you in a safe place? (PAUSE)

Are you fascinated by the power of the volcano? (PAUSE) Or do you want to leave as quickly as you can? (PAUSE)

It's almost time to go. (PAUSE) You realise you have your anxieties in your rucksack. (PAUSE) They are weighing heavily on your shoulders. (PAUSE) Will you open your rucksack and throw your anxieties one by one into the flow of lava, to be crushed into oblivion? (PAUSE) Or would you prefer to keep them? (PAUSE) The choice is yours.

When you are ready, return to the here and now and open your eyes. I invite you to create the colours of your experience during the visit to the volcano.

Objectives

The aim of *Volcanic Eruption* is, first, for clients to experience the emotions of watching the lava and fire and to be aware of the power in nature that is beyond their control. Second, it encourages clients to release their anxieties and allow the lava to carry them away.

Two apples

Materials needed

Paints, pastels, brushes, paper.

Instructions

The therapist leads the visualisation:

Get yourself comfortable and close your eyes if you want.

In your imagination see two apples in front of you. (PAUSE) Both are big, red and juicy looking. (PAUSE) One is unblemished. (PAUSE) The other has spots on the skin, a bruise or two and what looks like a worm hole. (PAUSE)

Which apple will you choose? (PAUSE) Do you value yourself enough to choose the better apple? (PAUSE) Or do you think the bruised one is all you are good enough to get? (PAUSE) Do you turn down the better apple so that someone else gets it? (PAUSE) Or do you choose the bruised one because that is what you usually get? (PAUSE)

What would it be like to choose the better apple because you are valuable? (PAUSE) That you are important? (PAUSE) That you matter? (PAUSE)

When you are ready come back into the room, open your eyes and paint your experience using the colours here.

Objectives

Many clients have low self-esteem that affects their choices in life. This visualisation enables clients to choose for themselves between two apples. It may seem an obvious choice. Will your clients choose the perfect apple or the bruised and marked one? Whichever they choose there is plenty of therapeutic potential to follow up that choice.

After the event

Materials needed

Paints, pastels, brushes, paper.

Instructions

The therapist leads the visualisation:

Close your eyes if you want to, relax and be ready for a visualisation.

It's morning. You wake up and look at your arm. You are wearing a wristband from some event. (PAUSE) Memories come flooding back. (PAUSE) Where did you go? (PAUSE) What did you do? (PAUSE)

Was it something you had been looking forward to for a long time? (PAUSE) Or something you dreaded? (PAUSE) Was it a planned event? (PAUSE) Or one that was on the spur of the moment? (PAUSE)

Did you go with friends? (PAUSE) Or were you alone? (PAUSE)

Where did you go? (PAUSE) Was it a good time? (PAUSE) Or did you consider it a waste of time? (PAUSE)

Was it an enjoyable event? (PAUSE) Or did things turn out badly? (PAUSE)

Your wristband continually reminds you. (PAUSE) Will you keep it on to mark a special event? (PAUSE) Or will you cut it off and throw it in the trash along with the memories you would rather forget? (PAUSE)

It's your choice. (PAUSE)

When you are ready come back into the here and now, open your eyes and use colours to express your experience from this visualisation.

Objectives

This visualisation can be used to help clients look back at something in their past. The aim is to get them to think about that 'something' and to consider whether it was good or bad, useful or unhelpful. Perhaps it was a mixture? Clients have a choice to move on and leave aspects of the past behind, keep the armband of that experience or hold on to only certain aspects. It is their choice.

A child of your choice

Materials needed

Paints, pastels, brushes, paper.

Instructions

The therapist leads the visualisation:

Get comfortable and close your eyes if it helps.

You are facing a row of children of different ages. (PAUSE) They are all the same gender as you. (PAUSE) As you look closer you realise with astonishment that each of them is you at a different age and stage in your childhood. (PAUSE)

Look at them again. (PAUSE) As you look think about their ages. (PAUSE) Which ages come first to your mind? (PAUSE) Of those, can you think of one that is particularly special to you? (PAUSE) You don't need to know why. The child just needs to be special to you. (PAUSE)

Now take that child in your arms, embracing him or her as you would another child of that age. (PAUSE) Think about the child's positive qualities. (PAUSE) Strategies for survival and getting his or her needs met. (PAUSE) Without the child you are now embracing you wouldn't be the person you are today. (PAUSE) You might not even be here. (PAUSE) He or she has enabled you to reach the age you are now. (PAUSE)

Quietly say thank you to that child. (PAUSE) Enjoy his or her resourcefulness. (PAUSE)

As you embrace the child let him or her become a part of you. (PAUSE) Let that little hero become a part of you, now, at your age. (PAUSE)

When you are ready, return with your child to the here and now, opening your eyes. Using the paints, create colours to represent that hero inside of you, that child who enabled you to survive and get your needs met.

Objectives

Clients in this activity are invited to look at themselves as a child of a particular age and to find positives about that child, such as the decisions the child made that helped the client survive. In a sense it is helping clients to look for the hero inside themselves. In transactional analysis, the Child ego state consists of a Child at each age and stage of development. Looking at another approach, based on the inner child, John Bradshaw writes: 'As you allow your child to become an integral part of your life . . . a new power and creativity begin to emerge. You will connect with a fresh vision of your child, enriched and deepened by your years of adult experience' (Bradshaw, 1990, page 250).

The vision expressed

Introduction

Drama can be a powerful and effective addition to the use of visualisation. When clients move around the room using their bodies, on their own or in a group, it can be a way of releasing feelings and thoughts.

Drama can help to highlight situations or problems and enable the client to make sense of them. Drama therapist Dr Sue Jennings writes: 'Drama can help all of us, if we choose to explore its potential' (Jennings, 1986, page v).

Jennings spent many years researching and developing the theory of drama therapy known as EPR – Embodiment, Projection, Role (for example, Jennings, 2003). She calls this model 'dramatic child development' and most therapeutic drama can be identified as being in one of these stages. We see it as linking with Pam Levin-Landheer's child developmental model (Levin-Landheer, 1982).

Embodiment

The first stage is the *Embodiment* phase, described by Levin as *Being*. This takes place during the first six months of life. The child is closely bound to his or her primary carer – usually mother. Jennings goes even further back and says that it starts before birth in the dramatised relationship between the mother and the unborn baby.

During the Embodiment phase the child starts to explore basic movements, physical contact, the five senses and simple ways of coping with life. He or she remains helpless and at the Being stage.

The client who has elements missing from that stage of development may find it helpful to do large body movement activities. He or she may enjoy singing games, especially those involving activities such as touching head, knees and feet. He or she will appreciate activities to develop coping strategies, such as crossing a river on pretend stepping stones, avoiding crocodiles and piranha as he or she crosses.

Projection

Movement from the Embodiment to the Projection stage is usually marked by what Donald Winnicott calls the 'transitional object'. It is often a piece of cloth or a teddy bear and its smell and texture is linked to the child's sensory experience in close contact with his or her primary carer.

In the Projection stage – similar to the Thinking and Doing stages from Levin (six months to three years) – the child starts to respond to the world around him or her. The child may use crayons or paints, for instance. Gradually he or she starts to relate objects to each other. The child might construct buildings from blocks. Then he or she starts to use stories through toys and puppets. This projection is gradually replaced by *being* the toys or puppets themselves.

Having available hand puppets and dressing-up clothes can be useful for clients of all ages who need to revisit this stage.

Role

The child moves into the Role phase of dramatic child development (known as the Identity and Skills stages of Levin – six to 12 years). Often there is another object of transition, in this case a stick or sword or a particular costume of authority. The child becomes the director of the play as well as the actor in it.

This is the stage where the child performs many different plays relating to everyday life. In therapy the client (adult or child) at this stage naturally works through issues using a rich variety of skills and techniques.

People continue to revisit these areas through their developing years and into adult life. Amazingly, people even take up jobs and hobbies based on one of the three focuses!

Jennings again: 'Remember that creativity is catching, if you can feel creative and spontaneous and, above all, hopeful, your clients will also experience this' (Jennings, 1986, page vi).

Your life on film

Materials needed

Clothes and other props to enhance the drama.

Instructions

The therapist leads the visualisation:

I invite you to get comfortable and to close your eyes, if you would like.

Imagine you are at the cinema. (PAUSE) 3D. (PAUSE) Surround sound. (PAUSE) High definition. (PAUSE) Perhaps digitally remastered. (PAUSE)
 The film of your life comes on screen. (PAUSE) What kind of a film is it? (PAUSE) A romance? (PAUSE) A tragedy? (PAUSE) A thriller? (PAUSE) A comedy? (PAUSE) Action? (PAUSE) Science fiction? (PAUSE)
 As the story unfolds before you, how do you feel? (PAUSE)
 What are the recurring themes of the film? (PAUSE)
 The film is now three quarters of the way through. The projector breaks down. The screen goes blank and the lights come up. (PAUSE)
 How would you like your film to continue? (PAUSE) What will happen next? (PAUSE) What kind of outcome would you like it to be? (PAUSE)

Open your eyes, breathe deeply and come back into the room in the here and now. I invite you to act out the last part of your story in the new way you have decided. Use the whole therapy room, moving around in the way you would like.

Objectives

This visualisation follows the story of the client's life. The therapist needs to be particularly sensitive as the first part could be very painful for some clients. The film continues to outline the client's story. Encourage clients to look for positives in their lives. Help them then to make redecisions so that the end of the film will be a triumph instead of a tragedy. A redecision is a 'replacement of a self-limiting early decision by a new decision that takes account of the individual's full adult resources' (Stewart & Joines, 1987, page 333).

A bus journey

Materials needed
Clothes and other props to enhance the drama.

Instructions
The therapist leads the visualisation:

Get comfortable, closing your eyes if you want to. We are going on a bus journey.

What kind of bus is it in your imagination? (PAUSE) A long distance bus or a local one? (PAUSE) A single decker or a double decker? (PAUSE) A modern bus or one that is old-fashioned? (PAUSE)

Who are you on the bus? (PAUSE) The driver? (PAUSE) A ticket inspector? (PAUSE) A passenger? (PAUSE)

If you are a passenger, think about what kind of person you are. (PAUSE) A businessman? (PAUSE) A mother? (PAUSE) A child? (PAUSE) A baby? (PAUSE) A pensioner? (PAUSE) Someone else? (PAUSE) Are you travelling alone? (PAUSE) Or with someone else? (PAUSE)

Where are you going? (PAUSE) Business? (PAUSE) Pleasure? (PAUSE) Shopping? (PAUSE) Escape? (PAUSE) Are you looking forward to getting there? (PAUSE) Or dreading it? (PAUSE)

How are you feeling about the journey? (PAUSE) Are you relaxed? (PAUSE) Happy for the bus to take its time? (PAUSE) Or anxious? (PAUSE) Impatient? (PAUSE) Annoyed at the amount of traffic and number of red lights the bus is having to stop for? (PAUSE) Worried? (PAUSE) Afraid? (PAUSE)

Are you travelling in silence? (PAUSE) Or are you speaking to others? (PAUSE) Are you reading to avoid contact? (PAUSE) Or are you eagerly looking to join in any conversation? (PAUSE)

The bus is slowing down. It's time to get off. How do you feel about leaving the bus? (PAUSE)

When you are ready, open your eyes and come back into the room. Now, using your creative imagination recreate the bus journey using drama. Be aware of your feeling and thinking as you make the journey.

Objectives
This visualisation is a journey of discovery in which clients are invited to think about their role in life. They will hopefully consider how they interact with the world around them. When clients have worked through this visualisation and drama they may decide to change their role to a more effective one.

Call the lifeboat

Materials needed

Clothes and other props to enhance the drama.

Instructions

The therapist leads the visualisation:

Get yourself comfortable and close your eyes if you would like to.

It started as a jolly trip with family or friends on a sunny afternoon. (PAUSE) Who was rowing? (PAUSE) Was it fun to be in a boat with people you like to be with? (PAUSE) Were you anxious or carefree? (PAUSE)

Water began to seep in through the wooden boards. (PAUSE) How did you react? (PAUSE) What did you do? (PAUSE) One of the party was feeling ingenious and suggested using their sun hat to bail out the water. What did you think? (PAUSE) How did you feel? (PAUSE) What did you do? (PAUSE)

Soon it was getting serious and the sea a little choppy. (PAUSE) Who decided to call the Coastguard? (PAUSE) What happened while you were waiting for the lifeboat? (PAUSE) Did you feel like abandoning ship and swimming back to the beach? (PAUSE) Did you think you would drown within clear sight of land? (PAUSE) How was the atmosphere within the group? (PAUSE)

The lifeboat has arrived. You are helped to climb aboard. (PAUSE)

You are in the lifeboat with your friends or family. (PAUSE) You have been rescued from the leaking rowing boat just off the coast. (PAUSE) How are you feeling? (PAUSE) What are you thinking? (PAUSE) How do you feel about the hire company for renting you an unseaworthy craft? (PAUSE)

The lifeboat comes back to the lifeboat station with thanks all round. (PAUSE) You climb up the steps and go back to the beach. (PAUSE)

When you are ready open your eyes and become a landlubber again. Now use drama to recreate your own experience in the lifeboat.

Objectives

This dramatic visualisation follows the story of a boat in trouble. A lifeboat is called. The scene takes the client through thinking and feeling to action. Also included are elements of trust and relationship.

Carnival parade

Materials needed

Clothes and other props to enhance the drama.

Instructions

The therapist leads the visualisation:

Get comfortable and close your eyes if you want to.

Imagine you are waiting for the carnival parade. (PAUSE) You are standing in a crowd at the edge of the pavement. (PAUSE) Some people are pushing. (PAUSE) How do you feel? (PAUSE) What do you think? (PAUSE) What, if anything, do you want to do about it? (PAUSE)

Gradually, you start to hear the music, long before the band arrives. (PAUSE)

Excitement mounts. (PAUSE) You lean forward to see colour and flamboyant headdresses. (PAUSE) The floats come into view. (PAUSE) You are engulfed in noises, sights and smells. (PAUSE) How do you feel? (PAUSE) Are you dancing? (PAUSE) Clapping? (PAUSE) Smiling? (PAUSE) Laughing? (PAUSE) Or do you withdraw to the back of the crowd? (PAUSE)

Many police are marshalling the event. (PAUSE) Does that help you to feel secure? (PAUSE) Or do you feel threatened? (PAUSE)

One of the people in the procession is giving things away. (PAUSE) They are just what you need. (PAUSE) You reach forward and take one of them. (PAUSE)

The parade dances its way towards its destination. (PAUSE) The excitement dies down. (PAUSE) The parade is over. (PAUSE) You are left with something you needed in your hand. (PAUSE)

Be aware of what you have in your hand. (PAUSE) What does it feel like? (PAUSE) How will it help? (PAUSE)

When you are ready, come inside to the here and now, bringing your object with you, and open your eyes. Now, dramatise your experience of the carnival parade, using the object in your hand if you want.

Objectives

Clients are invited to be involved in the *Carnival Parade* as much as they want to be. Towards the end of the scenario something is offered. It is just what the client needs. The client is encouraged to receive this free gift and take it forward in life.

Lost in the forest

Materials needed

Clothes and other props to enhance the drama.

Instructions

The therapist leads the visualisation:

Get comfortable and close your eyes if you want to. We are going to a large forest.

It's dark in the forest. (PAUSE) Dusk has given way to night. (PAUSE) You can only just make out the ghostly shapes of the tree trunks. (PAUSE) There is hardly a sound. (PAUSE)
　　You are alone and lost. (PAUSE) When you came into the forest, the sun was shining and the birds were singing. (PAUSE) It seemed like a pleasant stroll at the time. (PAUSE) You thought you would easily find your way out again. (PAUSE) But you just can't find the way. (PAUSE)
　　What is it like being lost? (PAUSE) What is going through your mind? (PAUSE) How are you feeling? (PAUSE)
　　You search and search. (PAUSE) There just doesn't seem a way out. (PAUSE)
　　Then you spot it. (PAUSE) A tiny light in the dim distance. (PAUSE) You move towards it. (PAUSE) As you get closer the light seems to shine brighter. (PAUSE) Finally, when you have almost reached the light, you notice the road leading out of the forest. (PAUSE) How do you feel? (PAUSE) What is going through your mind? (PAUSE) What will you do now? (PAUSE)

Follow the road out of the forest and back into this room, opening your eyes. Now I invite you to dramatise your experience of being lost in the forest, seeing the light and finding your way to safety.

Objectives

This descriptive visualisation is about a journey from being lost to discovering a way out of the forest. Clients are invited to make a decision. Will they stay lost or continue towards the road and finding their way forward?

Lone navigation

Materials needed

Clothes and other props to enhance the drama.

Instructions

The therapist leads the visualisation:

Get comfortable and close your eyes if you want. We are going sailing.

Imagine you are at the tiller of a 75-foot yacht. (PAUSE) You are sailing singlehanded across uncharted waters. (PAUSE) What is your yacht called? (PAUSE) How do you feel? (PAUSE)

Where in the world are you? (PAUSE) A good place? (PAUSE) A bad place? (PAUSE) Dangerous? (PAUSE) Desolate? (PAUSE) A place of beauty? (PAUSE) Peaceful? (PAUSE)

The weather is fair and everything seems under control. (PAUSE) You look out at the view of the vast ocean. (PAUSE) Are you lonely? (PAUSE) Afraid? (PAUSE) Secure? (PAUSE) Confident? (PAUSE) Happy with your own company? (PAUSE)

Do you like this sense of isolation? (PAUSE) Being in charge of your own destiny? (PAUSE)

Some dolphins come alongside and swim with you for a while. (PAUSE) Are they welcome companions? (PAUSE) Or do they seem threatening? (PAUSE)

Hours pass and the view is the same. (PAUSE) Are you sure you are going the right way? (PAUSE) Or do you feel panicky, desperate for some reassurance that your compass reading is correct? (PAUSE)

Evening comes. (PAUSE) There is a beautiful sunset. (PAUSE) You pause to take photographs. (PAUSE) Then darkness falls. (PAUSE)

It quickly becomes cold and the wind picks up. (PAUSE) Waves splash against the yacht from all sides. (PAUSE) Your sailing craft is tossed in the inky-black water. (PAUSE) How do you feel? (PAUSE) What are you thinking? (PAUSE)

Using your night-vision goggles you see a land mass ahead. (PAUSE) You turn your yacht towards it. (PAUSE) Soon you are heading into the harbour. (PAUSE)

Tie up the ropes, step out of the yacht, open your eyes and come back into this room. Now, using your dramatic skills recreate your journey on the waves.

Objectives

This nautical story explores various feelings that would be experienced by a lone yachtsperson. It follows the triumphs and stresses of the trip, helping clients to think about their own coping strategies for life.

Helicopter trip

Materials needed

Clothes and other props to enhance the drama.

Instructions

The therapist leads the visualisation:

Close your eyes if you want to, get yourself comfortable and fasten your seatbelts. You are going on a helicopter trip.

Notice how loud it gets as the engine warms up. (PAUSE) Now the helicopter is lifting off from the helipad. (PAUSE) Notice the vibrations. (PAUSE) Do you feel safe and excited? (PAUSE) Or nervous and scared? (PAUSE) You rise higher into the air. (PAUSE)

Look down and see how much smaller everything appears. (PAUSE) Notice the patterns of the villages and fields. (PAUSE). It seems like a map below you. (PAUSE) You look closer and realise that below you is an outline of your life. (PAUSE) You can see gentle rolling hills, those happy times you have known. (PAUSE) There is rough, rocky landscape, marking troubles in your life. (PAUSE)

What is it like being above the problems and difficulties, rather than in the middle of them? (PAUSE) Do you have a different perspective? (PAUSE)

You look back and see what you have flown over. (PAUSE) You see the difficulties, but they are over now and you have survived. (PAUSE)

Now look at the present view. (PAUSE) What do you see? (PAUSE)

From your helicopter view, look at the hazy landscape ahead that is your future. (PAUSE) Are you hoping for smoother landscape ahead? (PAUSE) Or are you expecting more trouble? (PAUSE)

What have you learned from the past and present that will help you when you reach the future landscape? (PAUSE)

When you are ready, come back into the room and open your eyes. Using the visualisation as a guide, act out your life, showing your timeline from past to present to future.

Objectives

Helicopter Trip gives clients the chance to look at their life so far from a different perspective, 'thinking outside the box'. Eric Berne stressed the usefulness of objectivity for the client when he introduced the idea of 'Martian thinking' (Berne, 1972/65, page 129). Ian Stewart (lecture, circ 1996) took Berne's idea and introduced the 'helicopter view'. As clients look at their life from 'above' they have the opportunity to make new decisions.

Hidden treasure

Materials needed

Clothes and other props to enhance the drama.

Instructions

The therapist leads the visualisation:

Close your eyes if you want to, get comfortable and come with me to the beach.

Imagine you are on a fossil hunting trip. (PAUSE) There are many interesting fossils scattered around the beach. A few perfect ones lie in huge slabs of rock, too big to remove. (PAUSE)

You are absorbed in your work of collecting rocks. (PAUSE) You put them carefully in your bag. (PAUSE)

As you are looking around you notice something unusual. (PAUSE) It is buried deep and it takes a while to reach. (PAUSE) You move stones and scrape at the sand. (PAUSE) Sometimes you scratch your fingers. (PAUSE) But you carry on, determined to reach the unusual rock. (PAUSE)

Eventually, everything is out of the way. (PAUSE) You reach down to take this perfect fossil. (PAUSE) It fits neatly into your palm. (PAUSE)

How does it feel to have found such a treasure? (PAUSE) What will you do with it? (PAUSE)

You take it down to the water's edge. (PAUSE) You wash off the sand. (PAUSE) A big wave comes and almost snatches it out of your hand. (PAUSE) How does it feel almost to lose your treasure when you have so recently found it? (PAUSE)

Hold the fossil tightly and carefully. (PAUSE) Feel the ridges in the stone and marvel. (PAUSE) It has been in the ground for ages. (PAUSE) Waiting for you to find it. (PAUSE)

Enjoy it. (PAUSE) And treasure it. (PAUSE) Use it to make a difference in your life today. (PAUSE)

When you are ready, open your eyes, return to the here and now and dramatise your experience of the story of finding the perfect fossil.

Objectives

The objective of this visualisation is to explore what is important for clients. At the end clients may decide to take what they need to help them move forward.

NOTE FOR THERAPIST: Consider making a collection of interesting small stones or fossils so that each time you use this visualisation you can give your client one of them as a transitional object.

Collage and 3D creation

Introduction

Making a collage or developing a 3D model is a practical way to bring the visualisation to life.

Collage using textures, patterns and colours can be really significant for clients in their therapeutic journey.

3D and collage are abstract forms of art, allowing clients to give substance to their feelings and thinking.

When a client produces an abstract piece of art in response to the visualisation, it transcends the need for words and interpretation, using the creative rather than the thinking part of the brain.

It is important to have a range of materials available. Suggestions include liquid glue, glue stick and cellophane tape as well as glitter, sequins, beads, coloured papers, pieces of fabric, ribbon and textured card and paper. Small boxes and balloons are also useful. Ensure that you have plenty of different colours for each category. All these can be bought from stationers or craft shops.

The waterfall

Materials needed

Paper, glue, glitter, sequins, small boxes and other items for collage/3D.

Instructions

The therapist leads the visualisation:

Sit comfortably. Close your eyes if you want to. We are going for a walk in the countryside.

You are wearing boots and appropriate clothing for walking. You have a hiking stick in your hand. (PAUSE)

You begin your walk on a small path beside a stream. (PAUSE) The birds are singing. (PAUSE) There is a gentle breeze. (PAUSE) You can hear the water lapping over the stones. (PAUSE)

There are big trees growing almost to the water's edge. (PAUSE) The breeze is rustling the leaves. (PAUSE)

You are enjoying walking in the countryside. (PAUSE) It is quiet and restful, the only sounds coming from nature. (PAUSE)

You walk on and the path starts to get steeper. The stream has become stronger and narrower and the water is noisier. (PAUSE)

It's a good feeling to be by the river (PAUSE), watching the bubbling and splashing of the water. (PAUSE) Feel the dampness in the air. (PAUSE) Be aware of the power of nature. (PAUSE)

The walk has become more of a climb. (PAUSE) You step over rocks, becoming breathless and exhilarated. (PAUSE) You climb up the hill higher and higher. (PAUSE)

Soon the path becomes a flight of roughly made steps. You continue climbing. (PAUSE) Occasionally you look back to see how far you have come. (PAUSE)

One last corner and you see it. Breathtakingly beautiful, awesome and a little frightening. (PAUSE) The force and power of the waterfall. (PAUSE)

Stand still and take in the sight. (PAUSE) The noise. (PAUSE) The spray lingering in the air. (PAUSE) Look carefully into the spray to catch a sight of an iridescent rainbow in the sparkling water. (PAUSE) Breathe deeply and enjoy. (PAUSE)

When you are ready, open your eyes and come back into room. Remember to leave your muddy boots outside! Now recreate your own waterfall on a piece of paper using glitter, sequins or other collage materials, adding details as you want.

Objectives

The Waterfall is a relaxation exercise. The aim is to take the client on a walk of discovery. The visualisation is full of the sights and sounds of a waterfall, providing refreshment and relaxation. Who knows? The experience may encourage clients to go and experience a waterfall for themselves, real or in their imaginations.

Helium balloons

Materials needed

Balloons, glue, glitter, sequins, and other items for collage/3D.

Instructions

The therapist leads the visualisation:

Sit comfortably, close your eyes if you would like and experience this story.

A man is walking through life. (PAUSE) Every now and then he stumbles over a difficulty or problem and he takes a helium balloon. (PAUSE) The man feels he has to carry with him the balloon containing his troubles. (PAUSE)

When it is windy, the balloon pulls and tugs and it is difficult to walk straight. (PAUSE)

Over time, more struggles come into life and he has to carry more and more of these balloons. (PAUSE) Eventually, just a breeze is enough to lift the man off his feet and send him spiralling out of control. (PAUSE)

Yet, somehow, he can't simply let go of the balloons because they belong to him. (PAUSE)

The man struggles on. (PAUSE) He doesn't know what else to do. (PAUSE) Every now and then he is lifted off the ground, buffeted and bruised as he crashes into things. (PAUSE)

By this time, the man is desperate to get back in control of his life. (PAUSE)

One day he has had enough. (PAUSE) So he sits down at home and pulls all the balloons towards him. (PAUSE) He carefully examines each of them to see what they contain. (PAUSE)

Some are old problems that aren't really relevant anymore. (PAUSE) So he bursts those balloons. (PAUSE)

Others are more complex, so he puts them under the table to prevent them from floating upwards. (PAUSE)

When he is finished, the bunch of balloons is smaller and more manageable. (PAUSE) The troubles haven't gone entirely, but they are more controllable. (PAUSE)

The man gathers up the balloons under the table and puts them into a cupboard. (PAUSE)

Come back into the room, open your eyes and look around you. I invite you to sit quietly and think about your struggles. (PAUSE) Are there any problems that aren't really relevant anymore? (PAUSE) Are there some you can get rid of? (PAUSE) Look at your own bunch of balloons. (PAUSE) Is it any smaller? (PAUSE) Is there somewhere you can put the rest to look at later? (PAUSE)

I invite you to choose balloons to represent your struggles, problems and difficulties. Attach a piece of string to each one. Then make a label to represent every difficulty, attaching these to the strings of separate balloons.

Look at the labels. Are there some difficulties that aren't relevant anymore? Blow up these balloons and burst them in whatever way you want. Is your bunch of balloons smaller now? For problems you want to deal with later, consider leaving the balloons deflated and giving them to your therapist for you to deal with at a later date.

Objectives

Clients are often weighed down by troubles, problems and anxieties. This visualisation shows how so often these difficulties are gathered and held on to. The practical exercise involving balloons gives an illustration of how, if they want, clients can keep or let go of their accumulated difficulties.

Tickets, please

Materials needed

Glue, glitter, sequins, small boxes and other items for collage/3D.

Instructions

The therapist leads the visualisation:

Make yourself comfortable and close your eyes if you want to. You are going on a train journey.

You arrive at the station. (PAUSE) Is it a very busy city station, with people hurrying, pushing? (PAUSE) Everyone intent on getting to their destination? (PAUSE) Or is it a quiet station with only an occasional train and one or two other passengers? (PAUSE)
    You buy a ticket. (PAUSE) Is it a long or a short journey? (PAUSE)
    Find the platform and begin waiting for the train. (PAUSE) How are you feeling? (PAUSE) Excited? (PAUSE) Anxious? (PAUSE)
    The train arrives and you climb aboard. (PAUSE) What kind of a train is it? (PAUSE) A high speed train? (PAUSE) A local train calling at all stations? (PAUSE) A steam train full of tourists going on a scenic journey? (PAUSE)
    You climb aboard. (PAUSE) Can you find a seat? (PAUSE) Is it crowded? (PAUSE) Are you particular about where you want to sit? (PAUSE) Window seat? (PAUSE) Aisle seat ready for a quick escape? (PAUSE) Facing forward? (PAUSE) With your back to the engine? (PAUSE)
    Have you brought lots of baggage with you? (PAUSE) Or is it just one bag? (PAUSE) Is it difficult to stow away? Do you feel squashed or burdened with all these things you have brought with you for the journey? (PAUSE)

The doors have closed. (PAUSE) The guard waves his flag. (PAUSE) The train moves off. (PAUSE) Your journey has begun.

Where are you going? (PAUSE) Is someone going to meet you at the other end? (PAUSE)

The train speeds up. (PAUSE) Houses, factories, fields and farms flash past the window. (PAUSE) The train goes into a long tunnel. (PAUSE) It becomes dark outside the window. (PAUSE) The noise of the train seems to have changed. (PAUSE) Your ears could be popping. (PAUSE) What is being in the tunnel like for you? (PAUSE)

The rhythm of the train continues. (PAUSE)

An inspector comes through the carriage to check the tickets. (PAUSE) You look for your ticket. (PAUSE) Are you anxious that you may have lost it? (PAUSE) Or bought the wrong ticket? (PAUSE) The inspector moves along the carriage and it is quiet. (PAUSE) How are you feeling? (PAUSE)

Your station is announced over the intercom. 'The next station we are arriving at is . . . (PAUSE) Please remember all your baggage. (PAUSE) And mind the gap as you leave the train.' (PAUSE)

The train stops. (PAUSE) You open the door and step down on to the platform at your destination. (PAUSE) How are you feeling now? (PAUSE)

When you are ready, climb the steps to leave the station and come back to the near and now. Using the materials here, I invite you to create a collage or 3D image of your personal train journey.

Objectives

This visualisation is full of choices, making the experience unique for each individual. Clients can make their own journey and travel to their own destination. Creating a collage/3D can enhance the experience and encourage the client towards deciding a new destination in life.

Buddies

Materials needed

Glue, glitter, sequins, small boxes and other items for collage/3D.

Instructions

The therapist leads the visualisation:

Get comfortable, close your eyes if you want to and join me in an underwater adventure.

Two divers are swimming through the ocean. (PAUSE) They are keeping in contact with one another using hand signals. (PAUSE) They are always aware of each other. (PAUSE) They are each looking out for the welfare of their diving buddy. (PAUSE)

I invite you to join the dive. (PAUSE) choose someone in your life to be your buddy. (PAUSE) How do you feel in the deep, dark water? What are you thinking? (PAUSE) What can you see? What do you hear? (PAUSE)

You and your buddy swim on, stopping to check that you have enough oxygen. (PAUSE) Then you see a shipwreck. (PAUSE) Submerged. (PAUSE) Dark. (PAUSE) Mysterious. (PAUSE)

It is covered with years of growth. (PAUSE) Seaweed. (PAUSE) Coral. (PAUSE) Barnacles. (PAUSE) Anemones. (PAUSE)

Are you excited by this discovery? (PAUSE) Or do you sense some kind of danger? (PAUSE)

You signal to your buddy. (PAUSE) What will you do now? (PAUSE) Your buddy is keen to continue exploring the shipwreck so you agree. (PAUSE) How do you feel? (PAUSE) Reluctant? (PAUSE) Enthusiastic? (PAUSE) Like an explorer? (PAUSE) Or as if you are being sucked into imminent danger? (PAUSE)

The shipwreck looks old, with a strange beauty. (PAUSE) Nature has taken over and made use of the rusting hull of the once majestic ship. (PAUSE)

As you explore, you wonder about the sailors and passengers. (PAUSE) What happened to cause the ship to sink? (PAUSE)

You signal to your buddy. (PAUSE) Your buddy is going in to take a closer look. (PAUSE) You follow. (PAUSE) How do you feel? (PAUSE) What are you thinking? (PAUSE)

In among the debris you see something glistening. (PAUSE) Making excited signals you alert your buddy. (PAUSE) Together you search using your hands to uncover the shining objects. (PAUSE) You discover two gold doubloons. (PAUSE)

Time is up. (PAUSE) Your oxygen levels are getting lower. You signal the thumbs up agreement to your buddy. (PAUSE) Together you swim to the surface, each clutching a gold coin. (PAUSE) How do you feel? (PAUSE) What are you thinking? (PAUSE) What will you do with your treasure? (PAUSE)

When you are ready, break the surface of the water, climb back into the boat, open your eyes and come back into the here and now. I invite you to create your own treasure using the craft materials here in the room.

Objectives

The scenario in this visualisation focuses on friendship and care for each other. It stresses the need to have close friends in life. The treasure of their choice clients find can help make a difference in their therapeutic journey. NOTE FOR THERAPIST: Consider buying some chocolate gold coins (the kind sold for Christmas) and giving two to your client as transitional (and delicious) objects.

Treasure!

Materials needed

Glue, glitter, sequins, small boxes and other items for collage/3D.

Instructions

The therapist leads the visualisation:

Get comfortable and close your eyes if you want. We are going treasure hunting.

You have found a very old map of a tropical island with a large X showing where the treasure is buried. (PAUSE) Your boat has just landed on the beach of the deserted island. (PAUSE) Are you excited? (PAUSE) Anxious? (PAUSE) Relaxed? (PAUSE) Afraid? (PAUSE)

With machete in one hand and spade in the other you find it difficult to hold your map. (PAUSE) You struggle through the undergrowth, cutting a path for yourself, going upwards towards the top of the island. (PAUSE) What can you see? (PAUSE) What can you hear? (PAUSE)

What is it like being in such as hot place? (PAUSE) What do you think about the dangers? (PAUSE) Are you worried about snakes? (PAUSE) Tropical diseases? (PAUSE) Or are you taking life as it comes? (PAUSE)

You notice an outcrop of rock and check your map. (PAUSE) Almost there. (PAUSE) You find a large round stone sticking out of the ground and measure 20 paces from it, as your map shows. (PAUSE) Then you start to dig. (PAUSE) The digging is very difficult because of the many roots. (PAUSE) You hack away with your machete and this helps you to use your spade on the soil. (PAUSE)

After what seems like hours your spade strikes something hard and metallic. (PAUSE) You have found the treasure chest! (PAUSE) You scrape away the soil around it and, with a mighty heave, you lift it out of the ground. *(PAUSE)* There is a strong padlock keeping it closed. *(PAUSE)* You bang hard with your spade. *(PAUSE)* Just when you are about to give up, the padlock breaks. *(PAUSE)* With some effort you manage to lift the lid. *(PAUSE)*

There it is. *(PAUSE)* The treasure you have always wanted. *(PAUSE)* You reach inside and take out the treasure, putting it in your bag. *(PAUSE)* Then you return to the beach and back into the boat. *(PAUSE)* Your mission has been accomplished. *(PAUSE)*

Now, climb out of the boat and back into the room. Open your eyes and create your treasure using the art materials here.

Objectives

The treasure chest in this story contains just what the client needs. Clients will have the opportunity to absorb the message of this visualisation and recreate their own treasure. *NOTE FOR THERAPIST: Consider collecting treasure (shells, stones, leaves) to give to clients after this scenario.*

An invitation

Materials needed

Glue, glitter, sequins, small boxes and other items for collage/3D.

Instructions

The therapist leads the visualisation:

Get comfortable, with your eyes closed if you want to.

I invite you to imagine you have received an invitation. (PAUSE)
What is it for? (PAUSE) A wedding? (PAUSE) An anniversary? (PAUSE) A birthday party? (PAUSE) A reunion? Or is it something else? (PAUSE)
How do you feel? (PAUSE) Are you excited? (PAUSE) Nervous? (PAUSE) Do you feel special and important to be invited? (PAUSE) Do you feel loved? (PAUSE)
Who else will be going? (PAUSE) People you like to spend time with? (PAUSE) Members of the family you would rather not meet? (PAUSE) Or will you be among strangers? (PAUSE)
Do you feel under obligation to go? (PAUSE) Or are you happy to accept? (PAUSE)
Will you ignore the invitation and pretend it got lost in the post? (PAUSE) Or will you put the invitation on the mantelpiece for everyone to see? (PAUSE)

When you are ready, put the invitation down and come back to the here and now. I invite you to make an invitation of your choice using the craft materials here.

Objectives

An Invitation is written in such a way that each client will experience it differently. The scenario is full of choices that give the client the chance to move forward at his or her own pace on the therapeutic journey.

A trip to the beach

Materials needed

Glue, glitter, sequins, sand, shells, seaweed and other items for collage/3D.

Instructions

The therapist leads the visualisation:

Sit comfortably and close your eyes if you want to. Come with me. We are going to the beach.

Step outside of the car and climb over the sand dunes. (PAUSE) The sand is soft and sliding beneath your feet. (PAUSE) Feel the sharpness of the dune grass. (PAUSE) The wind is blowing. (PAUSE) You can feel the sand almost scratching your legs. (PAUSE) You can smell in the air the saltiness of the sea. (PAUSE)

The sky is blue, with clouds racing across it. (PAUSE) Your hair is blowing in the wind. (PAUSE) The gulls are wheeling overhead and calling loudly. (PAUSE) The waves are breaking on to the beach. (PAUSE)

You walk and slide down the sand towards the beach. (PAUSE) There is nobody else here. Just you and the elements. (PAUSE)

You wander down to the edge of the water. (PAUSE) You pick up interesting stones and shells as you walk. (PAUSE) You saunter along the water's edge. (PAUSE) The waves are lapping over your feet and ankles. (PAUSE) The water is cold and invigorating. (PAUSE)

You stroll to the end of the beach and find a place to sit. (PAUSE) Look at the view. (PAUSE) What can you see? (PAUSE) What can you hear? (PAUSE) What can you smell? (PAUSE) How do you feel being alone in nature? (PAUSE)

Breathe deeply, remember the sights, smells and sounds as you leave. (PAUSE) Take the memories with you.

Climb back over the sand dunes and return to the car. (PAUSE)

When you are ready, open your eyes and come back to the here and now. The task is to make a collage using sand, shells, seaweed and glitter to recreate your trip to the beach.

Objectives

This is a relaxation after many people's heart! What can be more relaxing than a trip to the beach? The visualisation takes the client through the stages of going to the beach, absorbing the sights, sounds and smell of the visit. Hopefully it will be a stress reliever. *NOTE FOR THERAPIST: Consider collecting shells or beach pebbles to give to your clients as transitional objects after this visualisation.*

Gift of life

Materials needed

Glue, glitter, sequins and other items for collage/3D.

Instructions

The therapist leads the visualisation:

Make yourself comfortable, relax and close your eyes if that helps you.

Imagine someone is giving you a gift that will help you in your life. (PAUSE) What will the gift be? (PAUSE) Who will give it to you? (PAUSE) How will you use it? (PAUSE)
Will it solve all your problems? (PAUSE) Will it be a catalyst to help you on your journey of life? (PAUSE)
Take the gift in your hands. (PAUSE) Hold it. (PAUSE) Accept the gift you have been given. (PAUSE) Use it to help you move on in life. (PAUSE)

When you are ready, open your eyes and come back into the here and now, bringing your gift with you. Now create your gift using the materials in the room, decorating it in any way you like.

Objectives

This is an exploration of the client's feelings. The scenario promotes self-acceptance, which is often very important for vulnerable clients. This visualisation can also be used for problem-solving, giving clients space to think about and make new decisions.

Shaping the visualisation

Introduction

Visualisation combined with human sculpting can be a very useful tool.

At the end of the visualisation clients are invited to sculpt their bodies into a shape. This encourages them to take the thoughts, feelings and ideas from the visualisation and put them into a body shape.

Examples of what a client might be saying through the sculpting are: 'This is how I would like to be' and: 'I will look like this when I have achieved my goal.'

Although human sculpting can be used effectively with individuals it is also very useful in group work. Members of the group need to negotiate their position in the human sculpture created and this can help with teambuilding, cooperation and developing effective relationships.

Body sculpting can help move clients on into the new reality of their lives.

Journey of life

Materials needed

None.

Instructions

The therapist leads the visualisation:

Close your eyes if you want to, get comfortable and think about these questions on your journey of life.

Where have you come from? (PAUSE)
What events have shaped your life so far? (PAUSE)
Where are you today? (PAUSE)
How do you feel about yourself right now? (PAUSE)
Where are you going? (PAUSE)
What are your plans for the future? (PAUSE) Short term? (PAUSE) Long term? (PAUSE)

Now imagine yourself a statue or sculpture and, remaining motionless, show where you are right now on your journey of life.

Objectives

This short yet dynamic visualisation takes a look at life past and present. It encourages clients to look back and see how life was, how it is now and how they would like it to be in the future. It gives the time and space for clients to think about their journey and the direction they are going.

Turmoil to relaxation

Materials needed

None.

Instructions

The therapist leads the visualisation:

Close your eyes if you want to and prepare yourself to take part in this visualisation.

Turmoil is agitation, trouble leading to difficulties, inability to think or act. And most of all, confusion. (PAUSE)
I know my panic is normal and I won't die from it. (PAUSE) I need to be aware of my body's reactions. (PAUSE) Heart pounding. (PAUSE) A tight chest. (PAUSE)
I will think slowly and positively. (PAUSE) I know logically that everything will return to normal in a few minutes. (PAUSE) I breathe deeply and slowly. (PAUSE) Reminding myself again that there is nothing I can do to stop this process. (PAUSE)
Patience. (PAUSE) Pause. (PAUSE) I wait. (PAUSE) All will be OK. (PAUSE)
Relax. (PAUSE) I practise relaxing. (PAUSE) Me taking charge and bringing my body under control. (PAUSE)
I take care of myself. (PAUSE) Eat regularly and well. (PAUSE) I avoid stimulants such as caffeine and energy drinks. (PAUSE) I rest in the evenings. (PAUSE) Relaxing music. (PAUSE) A soothing bath. (PAUSE) Followed by a milky drink. (PAUSE) Bed. (PAUSE) And sleep. (PAUSE) The best medicine to give me energy to face tomorrow. (PAUSE)

When you are ready, open your eyes and come back into the room. I invite you now to use your body to show the shape of relaxation.

Objectives

This is a visualisation specifically for people who suffer from anxiety and panic attacks. It is very practical, taking people through an imaginary panic attack. There is plenty of reassurance all the way through that these feelings will pass. Hopefully this will help to lessen people's fear of a panic attack.

A mighty oak

Materials needed

None.

Instructions

The therapist leads the visualisation:

An oak is one of the strongest trees in the Western world. In this visualisation I invite you to become an oak. Start by making yourself comfortable, closing your eyes if you want to.

Right now you are an acorn in the dark earth. (PAUSE) For months you have lain in the ground, dormant. (PAUSE) But things are starting to change. You have developed some tiny roots and a shoot. (PAUSE) As the shoot breaks through the surface be aware of how delicate and vulnerable it is. (PAUSE)

Now your roots are growing deeper, absorbing moisture and nutrients from the lush soil. (PAUSE) Your shoot has developed two leaves that are opening to the sun's rays. (PAUSE)

The months are passing and your stem has become a small trunk carrying several leaves. (PAUSE) Be aware of the competition for space around you on the forest floor. (PAUSE)

The years pass and you have become a little tree. Your leaves form a small canopy. (PAUSE)

Now several decades have gone by. (PAUSE) You are a substantial tree, standing tall and proud and strong in the forest. (PAUSE) From your branches thousands of acorns are being produced each year. (PAUSE) Be aware of your strength and your influence. (PAUSE)

You are a tall, strong oak tree, one of the most majestic trees in the countryside. (PAUSE) The long time of growth has been worth it.

You have arrived. (PAUSE)

When you are ready, open your eyes and return as a person to the room. I now invite you to use your own body to sculpt the oak at its various ages and stages, seeing what that is like for you.

Objectives

This visualisation follows an acorn's progress and growth into a mighty oak tree. The scenario shows growth, strength and, eventually, the influence of the oak as it sheds acorns to pass on to others. Through this story and sculpting at the end clients can explore their own journey and influence in a positive and, hopefully, fun way. *NOTE FOR THERAPIST: Consider collecting acorns and giving one to each client at the end of this visualisation. You could see this as a form of transitional object.*

On top of the world

Materials needed

None.

Instructions

The therapist leads the visualisation:

Get comfortable, closing your eyes if you want to.

Imagine you are in a wild and mountainous landscape. (PAUSE) You are standing on a high peak looking all around you at the view. (PAUSE) How do you feel? (PAUSE)

Are you alone? (PAUSE) Or with friends? (PAUSE) Maybe you are in a large group, just arrived in a coach. (PAUSE)

Is it noisy and companionable? (PAUSE) Or do you stand alone and silent in a hostile environment? (PAUSE)

Look around you. (PAUSE) The wind is blowing. (PAUSE) It is cold up here. (PAUSE) The sky is an icy blue. (PAUSE) Clouds are racing across, occasionally covering the peaks of the mountains in the distance. (PAUSE) There are no trees here; it is bleak and rocky. (PAUSE)

How do you feel? (PAUSE) What are you thinking? (PAUSE)

You see a few mountain goats below. (PAUSE) You are wondering what they are finding to eat in such sparse vegetation. (PAUSE) Do you envy them their freedom? (PAUSE) Or do you think they have a hard life? (PAUSE)

You look into the distance and see smaller mountains all around you. (PAUSE) You wonder how climbers could reach this height. (PAUSE) Did they feel exhilarated when they reached the top of the world? (PAUSE) Was it here, on this very spot, that they planted the flag from their country to mark their achievement? (PAUSE)

As you turn to leave, you notice you have brought your bag of troubles with you. (PAUSE) You consider putting the bag of troubles on the cairn and covering it with stones. (PAUSE)

Once you have decided what to do with your bag of troubles, walk down the track, out of the wind and back to the here and now, opening your eyes. Now, using your body make a shape to express your feelings while you were on top of the mountain.

Objectives
This is a different form of relaxation, on top of a mountain range, far from the routine of everyday life. Clients are given the chance to take in the sights and sounds and experience the feelings about this scene. Then, towards the end, they have the option to leave their troubles on the mountain top – or at least some of them. What will they decide?

At the party

Materials needed

None.

Instructions

The therapist leads the visualisation:

Make yourself comfortable and close your eyes if you want to. We're going to a party!

What kind of a party is it? (PAUSE) Reunion? (PAUSE) Family party? (PAUSE) Child's birthday? (PAUSE)
    Is the party inside? (PAUSE) Or outside? (PAUSE) Are there many people there? (PAUSE) Do you know all the people? (PAUSE) Or only some? (PAUSE) Are you alone among strangers? (PAUSE)
    How do you feel? (PAUSE) What are you thinking? (PAUSE) Will you make new friends? (PAUSE) Have interesting conversations? (PAUSE) Or will you stay in the background? (PAUSE) Sneak in the kitchen to immerse yourself in the dishes? (PAUSE)
    Will you stay till the end? (PAUSE) or excuse yourself and leave early? (PAUSE)
    After the party will you have happy memories? (PAUSE) Or sad and uncomfortable ones? (PAUSE)

When you are ready, open your eyes and come back into the room. Using your body, I invite you to sculpt different poses you might have adopted during the party. Are there any you would like to do differently? Sculpt those, too.

Objectives

This story takes the client through all the scenes of the party. Often people show aspects of their script at a party and enter the role they chose in childhood. In the visualisation clients answer questions and the party becomes their own. The scenario and sculpting promote self-awareness and could even help the client find new strategies for future social events.

A gift for me

Materials needed

None.

Instructions

The therapist leads the visualisation:

Make yourself comfortable, close your eyes if you want and get ready for a visualisation.

Someone hands you a box. (PAUSE) It is a gift. (PAUSE) Who is it from? (PAUSE) How do you feel? (PAUSE) It is a medium-sized box. What are you thinking? (PAUSE) Do you feel special? (PAUSE) Excited? (PAUSE) Or dreading what might be inside? (PAUSE)

You lift the lid. (PAUSE) The box contains just what you need to help you in your life. (PAUSE) Will you reach in and take what you need? (PAUSE) Or will you leave it for someone else, thinking you don't deserve it? (PAUSE)

Look at the gift. (PAUSE) Bring it with you if you would like. (PAUSE)

Open your eyes and come back into the room with your gift. I invite you to use your body to sculpt the gift.

Objectives

A Gift for Me is what everyone wants. Or is it? Some may choose not to accept the gift or want someone else to have it. Clients are invited to consider all aspects of the gift before deciding. Exactly what the gift is and who it is from are left for the client to decide. Learning to accept the gift could be a way of building the client's self-esteem.

Taking care of yourself

Materials needed

None.

Instructions

The therapist leads the visualisation:

Make yourself comfortable and close your eyes if you would like.

What would it be like if you were to take care of yourself? (PAUSE) How would you feel? (PAUSE) What would you think? (PAUSE) What would you look like? (PAUSE) How much energy would you have? (PAUSE)

What would you do to take care of yourself? (PAUSE) Eat well? (PAUSE) Sleep properly? (PAUSE) Relaxation? (PAUSE) Socialising? (PAUSE) Exercise? (PAUSE) Taking time to rest, recuperate and recharge your batteries? (PAUSE)

How would you pamper yourself? (PAUSE) What treats would you plan for yourself? (PAUSE)

Examples for women might include: *Facial. (PAUSE) A trip to the hairdresser's. (PAUSE) Manicure. (PAUSE) Fish pedicure. (PAUSE)*

Examples for men might include: *A trip to the gym. (PAUSE) Sports massage. (PAUSE) Restyling at the hairdresser's. (PAUSE) A swim and a sauna. (PAUSE)*

You are unique. (PAUSE) And you definitely deserve to take care of yourself. (PAUSE)

When you are ready come back into the room and open your eyes. With your body sculpt a pose to show how you will look when you are taking care of yourself.

Objectives

Many people struggle with taking care of themselves. This visualisation will help and challenge them to acknowledge their needs and to start taking care of themselves. After all, they *are* worth it!

The visitor

Materials needed

None.

Instructions

The therapist leads the visualisation:

Get comfortable and close your eyes if you want to.

Imagine that someone very important is coming to visit you. (PAUSE) The person can be from your past or present. (PAUSE) Are you looking forward to the visit? (PAUSE)

When you meet, will you shake hands? (PAUSE) Kiss? Or hug? (PAUSE) Or will you just say hello? (PAUSE)

What will you talk about? (PAUSE) Will it be a short visit? (PAUSE) Or will your visitor stay all day and join you for meals? (PAUSE)

What will the atmosphere be like? (PAUSE) Relaxed? (PAUSE) Companionable? (PAUSE) Strained? (PAUSE) Awkward? (PAUSE) Will you be able to say all the things you want to? (PAUSE)

What would you like to do together? (PAUSE) Relax at home? (PAUSE) Or visit places you have been longing to show them? (PAUSE)

When your visitor has gone, how will you feel? (PAUSE) Satisfied? (PAUSE) Happy? (PAUSE) Lonely? (PAUSE) Disappointed? (PAUSE)

How will you use this visit to help you move on in life? (PAUSE)

When you are ready come back into the here and now and open your eyes. Using your body create a still sculpture of how this imaginary visitor has impacted on your life.

Objectives

The visualisation goes through the scenario of receiving a visitor. The client listens and makes decisions about the kind of visitor and what happens. The client has control on the outcome and hopefully this will be of benefit in the future.

Sources and references

Allan, J (1992). *Inscapes of the Child's World.* Dallas, Texas: Spring Publications.

Berne, Eric (1975). *What do you say after you say hello?* London: Corgi. (Original work published 1972.)

Bradshaw, John (1990). *Homecoming: Reclaiming and championing your inner child.* London: Bantam Books.

Jennings, Sue (1986). *Creative Drama in Groupwork.* Bicester, Oxfordshire: Speechmark.

Jennings, Sue (2003). Embodiment - Projection - Role. *The Prompt,* Autumn 2003.

Levin-Landheer, Pam (1982). The cycle of development. *Transactional Analysis Journal, 12,* 2, pages 129-139.

Stewart, Ian, & Joines, Vann (1987). *TA Today: A new introduction to transactional analysis.* Nottingham: Lifespace Publishing.

West, Janet, 1992. *Child-Centred Play Therapy.* London: Edward Arnold.

Wilson, Kate, & Ryan, Virginia (2005). *Play Therapy: A nondirective approach for children and adolescents.* London: Bailliere Tindall. (Original work published 1992.)

Lightning Source UK Ltd.
Milton Keynes UK
UKHW051847021021
391572UK00005B/514

9 781511 452526